Prayer doesn't co His disciples to people into praye to the pasture! I've seen the impact on our MegaFest participants as he taught and demonstrated the tremendous power of prayer. His book *Just Pray* is an opportunity to saturate your life with effectual, fervent prayer! It's a must-read and then a must-do!

—BISHOP T. D. JAKES
FOUNDING PASTOR, THE POTTER'S HOUSE

John Hannah is a world leader in prayer who embodies the consecration, intention, and heart of a true prayer warrior. His words are surgical and echo God's heart. Anything he has to say about prayer is worth reading.

—DR. IRISHEA HILLIARD
SENIOR PASTOR, NEW LIGHT CHRISTIAN CENTER CHURCH

As a pastor for over fifty-two years, I can say without a doubt that prayer has been the key to success. This has been the case not only for my ministry but also for my personal life. Pastor John Hannah has done a phenomenal job of placing a clarion call to the next generation of prayer warriors who will bombard heaven. I encourage you to read *Just Pray*, and be blessed by this message and challenged to strengthen your prayer life.

—CHARLES E. BLAKE SR.
PRESIDING BISHOP, CHURCH OF GOD IN CHRIST

Reading *Just Pray* will be a life-changing experience! It is a must-read from my brother John Hannah, who embodies what it is to be a praying pastor and lead a praying church and a praying community. This book is a timely answer for the prevailing question "What do we do now?" Just pray!

—Wilfredo "Choco" De Jesús
General Treasurer, the Assemblies of God

JUST PRAY

JOHN F. HANNAH

CHARISMA HOUSE

Most Charisma House Book Group products are available at special quantity discounts for bulk purchase for sales promotions, premiums, fund-raising, and educational needs. For details, call us at (407) 333-0600 or visit our website at www.charismahouse.com.

JUST PRAY by John F. Hannah
Published by Charisma House
Charisma Media/Charisma House Book Group
600 Rinehart Road, Lake Mary, Florida 32746

Visit the author's website at https://johnfhannah.com.

Library of Congress Cataloging-in-Publication Data:
An application to register this book for cataloging has been submitted to the Library of Congress.
International Standard Book Number: 978-1-62999-953-1
E-book ISBN: 978-1-62999-954-8

21 22 23 24 25 — 987654321
Printed in the United States of America

To all my faithful 4:00 a.m.,
Friday night, and Saturday
devotional prayer warriors
—thank you!
Let's keep interceding!

CONTENTS

PART III: A LIFE OF PRAYER

FOREWORD

WHEN I FIRST met Pastor John Hannah several years ago in Chicago, I experienced something profound. As I saw him minister in the grace and power of the Holy Spirit, I recognized in him a man of integrity, brilliance, and dependence on the Holy Spirit. I was inspired to go deeper and stronger in my relationship with God and to see change both personally and corporately. But when I heard Pastor John speak on prayer and demonstrate it at a large conference in South Africa, I recognized that God had given him a "now" word for the church globally.

Pastor John Hannah carries an anointing and a message that is so critical for our times. Through the power of the Holy Spirit, Pastor John has built a significant, large, and influential church on the South Side of Chicago. Prayer is not just a message Pastor John speaks; it is not merely a method he uses. It is a lifestyle he models. Indeed, it is his life message. And through his deep relationship with God, he has seen God do phenomenal things. Through his ministry, teaching, and God-given revelation, hundreds of thousands of people have been impacted in Chicago and around the world. Australia also has felt the impact of his ministry through our Planetshakers Conference and through his impact on me personally and on many other pastors and leaders.

We are living in some of the most challenging times in modern history, and it is a great pity that at a time like this, when the church more than ever should be walking in obedience to God's command to "pray at all times in the Spirit" (Eph. 6:18, NASB), few of us are found in His presence. At a time like this, God is the person we should be calling upon and going deep with, because only He has the power to bring change to the chaos and turmoil.

We need so desperately to access God's power and love that come through prayer to bring change to our world. But there is an even greater reason that now, like never before, we just need to pray. I believe we are about to witness one of the greatest moves of God, if not *the* greatest move of God, the world has yet experienced. And prayer is the key. Every significant move of God has been precipitated and sustained through prayer. Prayer is God's invitation to intimacy. Prayer is heaven's open secret to accessing God's power. Prayer is the primary vocation of every Christian.

I believe this book will inspire you to seek the Father like never before. It will help you go deeper in your relationship with God and grow in your spiritual authority. It will give you the keys to seeing breakthrough and transformation in the world. It will bring an impartation of kingdom truth, which literally will change your life and the world around you. But more importantly, it will prepare you for what God is desiring to do in this generation. I pray that you will be impacted by the ministry of Pastor John Hannah as I was and as our church at Planetshakers was and continues to be.

When the disciples of Jesus witnessed His miraculous power to bring transformation, reformation, healing, and freedom, and realized that prayer was the key to Jesus' life and ministry, hunger prompted them to say, "Lord, teach us to pray" (Luke 11:1). I believe God is stirring that hunger again, and I commend you in your desire to learn afresh the power of prayer as you read this book. The revelation it contains will see heaven come to earth just as Jesus Himself prayed it would when He said, "Your kingdom come. Your will be done, on earth as it is in heaven" (Matt. 6:10, NASB). So let's put aside the worry, fear, and frustration. Lay it all at God's feet and watch Him manifest! Just Pray!

RUSSELL EVANS is the founder, senior pastor, and director of Planetshakers Ministries and Planetshakers Church and the president of Planetshakers College. He is also part of the global leadership of Empowered21 and a member of the Oral Roberts University board of trustees.

INTRODUCTION

A GLOBAL PANDEMIC. AN economic recession. Widespread national protests. Even fire tornadoes! When I first said, "I want to write a book on prayer," I had no idea 2020 would be so, well, 2020. I had no idea we would go through so much as a country and a church. I had no inkling whatsoever that as I talked about prayer and how much we needed to get back to the throne of God, it would feel as if the earth were shaking under our feet, as if Satan was trying his hardest to uproot us and shake us to our core.

My guess is you identified with Job at some point in 2020 (maybe you still do), as blow after blow came in such a concentrated time. For many of us, it seems as if the earth has been shaking under our feet for so long now that we don't even know what normal looks like anymore. Every day, we hear about a new struggle or obstacle in our world. That doesn't include what you're walking through personally—the loss of a loved one, a cancer diagnosis, children who have gone off the path, affairs, drug abuse, divorce, unemployment, the list goes on. How do we stand firm where we've been planted in the midst of so much turmoil?

How do we, as David said in the very first psalm, become like "a tree planted by the rivers of water, that brings forth its fruit in its season, whose leaf also shall not wither; and whatever he does shall prosper" (v. 3, NKJV)? David knew what he was doing when he made that comparison. The tree is firmly planted because beneath the surface its roots have formed an invisible connection with the water's moisture and minerals, which keeps the tree in place.[1] And the same thing happens to us when we connect with our Creator and Savior.

That's what I'm talking about in this book—getting to that point in our journey where our roots are deeply entrenched and grafted into the source of life. It's about getting to the point where our faith is unshakable regardless of what's happening around us, whether we're facing a worldwide cataclysmal event or our own personal pain that makes our hearts literally ache. But how do we get to that unshakable place with Christ?

In a world that seems bent on shaking us senseless, unshakable faith can come only through an intimate relationship with Jesus. And—don't miss this!—the key to that kind of deeply rooted, one-on-one relationship is *prayer.* Just prayer.

Let me say that another way because I want you to get this: if you want unshakable faith, you must have a prayer life that brings you to the feet of your Creator and Savior every day. You must tap into the direct line of communication we gained access to when Jesus died on the cross and the veil separating us from God's presence was ripped in two.

The beautiful thing about this creation-Creator relationship is that it's mutual. Your Creator and Savior *wants* to talk to you, and He desires for you to talk to Him. He wants us to listen to Him—and He desires to listen to us. I believe that with everything I have. It's one of the reasons I decided to write this book.

Learning to Pray

I'll be honest with you and admit that I haven't always felt this way. Growing up, I didn't believe prayer was essential. As a child, I remember hearing my grandmother pray, but prayer didn't really resonate with me until I was personally taught how to pray by people God providentially placed in my life.

> If you want unshakable faith, you must have a prayer life that brings you to the feet of your Creator and Savior every day.

I didn't even know I needed to be taught to pray until these people of prayer got hold of me. Actually, I think it was God who got hold of me. He just used willing vessels. What I discovered when I was taught to pray is that I wanted to pray more—and that prayer is essential to my relationship with God. A lot of us don't realize the importance of learning how to pray. We don't get the truth that when we know how to pray, it changes our lives. It changes how we talk to God—and how He talks to us. We assume that we should just pray, but even the disciples asked Jesus to teach them how to pray (Luke 11:1). Jesus didn't say, "You already know how to pray." He responded with what we can use as a model for when we talk with God. In chapter 3 we'll get into the details of learning to pray.

But I can tell you right now that if you read this book and walk away having learned nothing but the fact that prayer is our lifeline, I'll consider my time writing this well spent. I'm telling you, friend, we can't do this thing called life without prayer. I can't do it, and you can't do it. I've seen it over and over again in my ministry—people trying to do the work of ministry in their own strength. You can't do this on your own. Prayer—talking with God—must be paramount.

I've been leading New Life Covenant Southeast (NLCSE) on the South Side of Chicago for the last seventeen years. We were planted by New Life Covenant Church in northwest Chicago, then led by my friend and brother Pastor Wilfredo De Jesús, who is now general treasurer of the Assemblies of God. From day one at NLCSE, we've made prayer a priority. We've seen people healed through prayer. We've seen the Holy Spirit move through prayer. We've seen marriages restored, neighbors reconciled, and prodigal children return—all as a result of prayer.

TOUCHING THE HEART OF GOD

Why have we seen such dramatic fruit in ministry? It's because through prayer we touch the heart and mind of God. Think about that for a minute and let it really sink in. In your intentional time spent talking and listening to God, you touch the heart and mind of the Creator of the universe, the One who knit you together in your mother's womb. You touch the feet of your Savior, the One who took all your sins upon Himself and willingly died a physical and spiritual death so that you could have an intimate relationship with Him. You do all that through prayer!

You've probably known people who even after facing one trial after another are still at peace, still worshipping, and still praying. They're still so strong in Christ. Their lives have been shaken repeatedly, yet their faith is unshakable. I think about the Christians in North Korea who spent years in prisons that have been compared to the

Nazi death camp Auschwitz and come out still praising Jesus. It's almost as if they've touched something we haven't. That's what I want for my life. It's what I want for our church. It's what I want for *you*.

Through prayer we touch the heart and mind of God.

When I was writing this book, most countries had gone through at least two COVID-19 quarantines. We had seen more than one million coronavirus deaths around the globe. The world was in an economic recession. Racial injustices and issues of inequality had risen to a boiling point, and protests (both peaceful and violent) had broken out in hundreds of cities and towns. On top of that, the United States was polarized and politicized—divided in just about every way. But at New Life Covenant Southeast, we weren't participating in the panic and uncertainty. I kept focusing on everything God was doing, put my trust in Him, and determined to maintain my position in prayer.

We remained in prayer because I realized very quickly that if we weren't talking to God about everything that was swirling around us, we'd take out our fears, frustration, and confusion on ourselves and others. If you don't talk to God about what's happening in you and in the world around you, you'll take matters into your own hands. You'll be angry and spew that rage at the wrong time in the wrong situation. Hear me now because you need to get this: *the only thing that keeps us level minded—that keeps us abiding in the Holy Spirit—is the Holy Spirit.* As we talk to God, the Holy Spirit works in us and through us—and for us.

I love that. I love that God ripped the veil so that He,

the almighty, all-powerful God, could communicate with us—so He could have a relationship with us. If you haven't guessed it by now, that's what we're talking about here. Prayer is intimate relationship with Him. Notice that I'm not saying prayer is talking *to* God but *with* Him. Talking *to* God, or God talking to us, implies a one-way conversation. When you spend time with a friend or spouse, you're talking *with* that person in relationship. That's what I want for you—intimate relationship with your Creator and Savior. Communing with God every day is essential to having unshakable faith. You can't have a friendship or a marriage without talking or communicating with the person in some way. The bottom line is, when no one is talking or listening, there's no real relationship.

That may sound harsh, but it's difficult to argue against. It rings true in our earthly relationships and in our faith. God doesn't mince words in His commands to pray, because He knows it sustains and grows the relationship between Him and His people. And relationship with you is what God desires. That truth is revealed throughout Scripture. Here are just a few of the scriptures about prayer and the powerful connection it creates between God's heart and ours.

> For we do not have a high priest who is unable to empathize with our weaknesses, but we have one who has been tempted in every way, just as we are—yet he did not sin. Let us then approach God's throne of grace with confidence, so that we may receive mercy and find grace to help us in our time of need.
>
> —HEBREWS 4:15–16

> Watch and pray so that you will not fall into temptation. The spirit is willing, but the flesh is weak.
>
> —Matthew 26:41

> Do not be anxious about anything, but in every situation, by prayer and petition, with thanksgiving, present your requests to God.
>
> —Philippians 4:6

> And pray in the Spirit on all occasions with all kinds of prayers and requests.
>
> —Ephesians 6:18

Anyone who knows me knows I have a love affair with the Bible. God's Word has always taken me where I needed to go and showed me what I needed to see. I want that for you too, so I've loaded up these chapters with scripture. I'm sharing stories you probably didn't even know were in the Bible. I include details and facts that might have you saying, "Where did he get that?" It's all in the inerrant Word of God, where we find so much treasure and a map for our lives.

Prayer is intimate relationship with God. . . .When no one is talking or listening, there's no real relationship.

I'm also sharing reflection questions at the end of each chapter to help you take what you've just read and use it to examine your heart and current prayer life. My hope is you'll take time to transparently answer these questions for yourself first and then adapt them for a small group study on prayer. I would love nothing better than to see you put into practice what I've taught and then teach others what you've learned.

Are you ready to head out on this Bible-fueled journey with me to grab hold of this lifeline—this intimate relationship that we all so desperately need in our lives and in our world today? I think God is waiting for you. I think He can't wait to see you at His feet so He can lift up your head, fix His eyes on yours, and tell you to cast all your cares on Him—and just pray.

PART I

A NEW COMMUNICATION

Chapter 1

THE SIT-DOWN

Does God Really Want to Listen to Us?

When they had finished eating,
Jesus said to Simon Peter,
"Simon son of John, do you love me
more than these?"
"Yes, Lord," he said, "you know that I love you."
—John 21:15

I wonder what went through Peter's mind when Jesus asked him that question. There he was, defeated in every sense of the word. He boasted that he would never deny the Master he had walked with for three years. And what did he do? The first time someone accused him of knowing Jesus, he lied and said, "I don't know Him." Peter did this not just once but *three* times—just as Jesus said he would, just as Peter said he wouldn't.

Luke's Gospel says that after he denied Jesus the third time and the rooster crowed, "the Lord turned and looked straight at Peter" (Luke 22:61). I can imagine that look. Peter was racked with guilt, shame, and condemnation. He knew he'd messed up!

So he was back on a fishing boat, back to the life he'd led before that seminal day when Jesus said, "Follow me, and I will make you fishers of men" (Matt. 4:19, ESV). And who did Peter see? The Master he wronged.

What happened next tells us less about Peter and more about Jesus' love for His disciple—and His love for us—because Jesus arranged for what I call a "sit-down." After the resurrection, twice Jesus went to the place where the eleven disciples were gathered. Now, if I had been Peter, I would've been hiding in the corner with my head down like, "Ugh, man, did I let You down." We can only guess how Peter reacted when he saw Jesus because Jesus didn't address Peter those two times. He knew Peter needed more than a passing conversation; he needed a one-on-one sit-down.

That day on the shore with the fish waiting, Jesus had a specific message for Peter—one of forgiveness and restoration—and He wanted to speak those words to His disciple face to face. I can imagine the conversation: "Peter, you've lied; you've cursed; you've denied Me. Now let's talk." Jesus wanted to build up Peter's confidence and call him back to His work. Peter needed to be restored. He needed to ask forgiveness and be forgiven.

All of that needed to happen in what I call a good, old-fashioned sit-down. Communication is more than just talking. It's also listening. In Peter's situation, he not only got to talk; he also got to listen. He had the privilege of communicating with God. He got to hear how much Jesus loves him, and he was able to tell Jesus, his Master and Lord, "I'm sorry. I love You." That's not a drive-through conversation. That's a sit-down!

There's such a difference between the drive-through and the sit-down experience. In a drive-through, you stay in the car, pull up to the window, order your food, pay, and leave. You don't go inside. You never sit down. The drive-through is instant; it has no time for patience. You want what you want *now.* The drive-through is the enemy of endurance.

But a sit-down meal at a restaurant offers the complete opposite experience. You get to enjoy the ambiance. You get to read a menu and see the many options. You may order an appetizer, an entrée, and dessert. You get to know the server and most importantly, you get to sit with a person or group and spend time talking and getting to know them and building your relationship.

> Peter was able to tell Jesus, his Master and Lord, "I'm sorry. I love You." That's not a drive-through conversation. That's a sit-down!

Remember during the COVID-19 quarantines when the restaurants were closed and you couldn't sit inside? If we wanted to eat out, our food options were delivery or drive-through. I missed restaurants so bad. I missed reading a menu, sitting across from my wife or a friend, and enjoying the ambiance. I missed eating on a plate with real silverware instead of out of a Styrofoam box. The sit-down is an entirely different experience, and it's where relationship deepens and grows.

The miracle of Jesus feeding the five thousand in Matthew 14 was another sit-down. The huge crowd was hungry, and like most of us do when we get hungry, they were complaining. (Picture five thousand grumbling, irritable people.) They were hangry. (Yes, that's a real word, newly added to the dictionary in 2020.) The disciples wanted to send them back into the city to get something to eat, but Jesus had compassion on the crowd. And just as you would expect, Jesus told His disciples, "You give them something to eat" (v. 16).

Then Jesus gave a generous boy the opportunity to be part of a story that He knew would be told billions of times two thousand years later. He took the boy's five tiny barley loaves and two fish—all he had—and multiplied it! Then Jesus hosted one of the biggest sit-downs in Scripture. He divided the hungry crowd into groups and directed the people to sit on the grass. He wanted them to take it all in. They needed to see Him break the bread. They needed to hear Him pray and thank God for the food He had provided.

> Taking the five loaves and the two fish and looking up to heaven, he gave thanks and broke the loaves.
>
> —John 14:19

And after they saw what prayer sounds like, they got to enjoy and be amazed by the results: miraculous nourishment for their growling stomachs and the overflow of twelve baskets of food after everyone got their fill. They needed to experience what was happening. They needed to realize exactly who they were with and that He was performing yet another miracle in their midst. So much can happen in a sit-down.

Here's the amazing takeaway from these stories. Are you ready? Just as Jesus went to great lengths to have a sit-down with Peter and the multitude of five thousand, *Jesus wants a face-to-face sit-down with you.* He wants to talk with you often and regularly. Talking with God only when you want something is a drive-through conversation. Just give me this, and I'll move on. God desires to know us and for us to know Him. He desires intimacy; He longs for relationship. He wants a sit-down, face-to-face conversation with each one of us every day—not just with me or your pastor or the prayer leader at your church. Jesus wants a sit-down, face-to-face conversation often and regularly—with *you*.

He's *That* Into You

In my teen years, when I first became a believer, I felt the need to consistently communicate with Jesus. I remember reading God's warning to Adam and Eve in Genesis 2—"The day you eat of this tree, you will surely die"—and about the separation between God and man that resulted when Adam and Eve believed Satan's lies over God's word. The lines of communication were cut. But I remember being so thankful that Christ came to reconnect us. I think of it like a telephone pole. If something's wrong with the phone line, you have to call someone to climb the pole to fix the connection. That's what Christ did. He climbed the cross to fix our relationship. That's how much God wants to talk with us.

> Jesus wants a sit-down, face-to-face conversation often and regularly—with *you*.

God loves us so much that He gave His only Son to be sacrificed on a cross so that we could have direct communication with Him and He could have direct communication with us. He created us because He wanted relationship. Genesis tells us that each day God walked the garden because He wanted to talk with His creation. When He called out for Adam—"Where are you?" (Gen.

3:9)—it was because up until then He had been dialoguing with Adam and Eve. He knew their voices, and they knew His. The man and woman were the only creations to whom He gave His breath.

> God loves you so much that He gave His only Son to be sacrificed on a cross so that you could have direct communication with Him.

Then everything was exposed. And that very day, God put the ultimate plan in motion to restore the relationship between Him and His creation—a sacrificial plan that would unfold at just the right time. Until then, the blood of animals would need to be shed. And intercessors would be needed—they would be the only ones allowed in the temple, and they would be separated from God's presence by a thirty-foot, ceiling-to-floor veil. For centuries, those intercessors, the priests, talked to God on behalf of the people. But that wasn't good enough for God. He actually created a way for us to return to Him and fellowship with Him. The moment Christ drew His last breath on the cross, God immediately ripped the temple veil from top to bottom. The earth literally shook that day.

The world has painted a picture of a faraway God who just sits on a throne. But that's not the God that Peter, Moses, and Paul knew—the God who spoke to them face to face. The God we serve, worship, and pray to is a loving, compassionate, and concerned Father. Paul called Him Abba Father: "Because you are his sons, God sent the Spirit of his Son into our hearts, the Spirit who calls out, 'Abba, Father'" (Gal. 4:6).

Jesus says there's no comparison between the love and care of a parent and God's love for us: "If you then, though you are evil, know how to give good gifts to your children, how much more will your Father in heaven give the Holy Spirit to those who ask him!" (Luke 11:13). For some of us, the idea of a good and perfect father is hard to comprehend. We never really saw it modeled. I get that. Both my mother and father were high school dropouts. My mother got pregnant with me when she was sixteen or seventeen. I was born into poverty. Growing up in the Chicago projects, drugs were part of our community. My father had gone to prison, but when he got out, I visited him on the weekends. He kept marijuana around the house and taught me how to smoke it when I was just a kid. The word *father* didn't exactly make me think of goodness and generosity.

But I'm here to tell you that you have a God, a Father, who's into you! He's into hearing your voice. He's so into you that in Luke 12:7, Jesus Himself says that He knows the very number of hairs on your head. He's so into you that He knows what you need, when you need it, even before you need it. But because He desires to talk with us, He tells us to pray. He knows the relationship is more important than our needs.

I think about Hezekiah and how God sent the prophet Isaiah to tell him to get his house in order because he wasn't going to recover from the festering boil on his skin; he was going to die. When Hezekiah heard this, he turned his face to the wall and started talking to God, reminding Him of their relationship.

> Remember, LORD, how I have walked before you faithfully and with wholehearted devotion and have done what is good in your eyes.
>
> —2 KINGS 20:3

God responded by telling Isaiah to "go back and tell Hezekiah…'I have heard your prayer and seen your tears; I will heal you'" (2 Kings 20:5). God gave Hezekiah fifteen more years on earth. Now *that's* an amazing relationship, right? And it's the same face-to-face, intimate relationship our God wants with us because He's *that* into us. He even monitors our tears.

> You keep track of all my sorrows. You have collected all my tears in your bottle. You have recorded each one in your book.
>
> —PSALM 56:8, NLT

God longs for a deep level of intimacy with you. Look where He wanted to be placed among the Israelites. When God told Moses to build the tent of meeting—the place of intimacy where Moses would go to talk to God—God said, "Set Me in the middle of the camp of the children of Israel." (See Numbers 2:17.) He wanted to be set in the middle of the twelve tribes, like a Father surrounded by His children.

> You have a God, a Father, who's into you! He's into hearing your voice. He knows the very number of hairs on your head.

Believe it or not, we serve a God who knows us and wants us to know Him. I realize it may not seem like that when the world is shaking and the fires are raging around you. But you can be absolutely sure that God wants you to hear Him and He wants to hear you. He wants you to know His Word, to know His promises—and to know His heart. In the Book of Acts, Luke wrote:

> His purpose was for the nations to seek after God and perhaps feel their way toward him and find him—though he is not far from any one of us. For in him we live and move and exist. As some of your own poets have said, "We are his offspring."
>
> —Acts 17:27–28, NLT

I'm *begging* you to get that. I'm praying you understand that this same God (remember, He is the same yesterday, today, and tomorrow) is your Father, just as Acts 17 tells us. He wants this kind of intimacy with you. He yearns to be smack-dab in the center of your life and heart. He wants you to truly see Him, to genuinely know Him, to honestly talk with Him. And He wants to spend that kind of time with you every day. He's *that* into you.

In the Face of God

So how do we get to this place of intimate relationship, where we develop unshakable faith? I'm here to tell you that this kind of intimacy and faith come only through prayer, through communication. When we talk with God, we can seek His face. *Through prayer, we get in the face, in the presence, of our God.* I love picturing God and Moses together. Exodus 33:11 tells us that "the Lord would speak to Moses face to face, as one speaks to a friend." That is *so* good. I love the fact that the same God who walked with Moses and spoke with him face to face wants to commune with you and me. He wants to fellowship with you.

But I want you to notice something. I want you to see that these intimate relationships between God and Moses, between God and Hezekiah, between Jesus and Peter—they didn't just automatically materialize. They were cultivated through walking with God, listening to Him, loving Him, and seeking His face. Think about your relationships with your spouse or a best friend. You didn't have the intimacy you do now when you met the person for the first time. It takes quantity and quality time, special moments, listening, and obedient action to build intimacy and trust. Relationship deepens with time spent communicating with each other.

> Your Savior and Creator yearns to be smack-dab in the center of your life and heart.

Before I proposed to my wife, Anna, I spent time with her. The more I talked with her, the more I got to know her and the more comfortable I became around her and in our relationship. As I found myself wanting to spend more and more time with her, I knew she was my partner in life. Now that we've been married twenty-eight years, I've realized even more about her, like the fact that she always wants the best for me. Our relationship and intimacy have deepened and grown even sweeter. But it didn't happen overnight. No way. Far from it.

It's the same in our relationship with Christ. As we spend time with Him through prayer and worship—talking honestly with Him, thanking Him, and sharing every part of our heart—our love for Jesus grows. The more time we spend with Him, the more we will want to seek His face.

The beautiful thing is that as we seek Him, He moves closer to us. My grandmother always told me, "Draw nigh to God, and He will draw nigh to you." I love that promise in James 4:8. It's a picture of two-way communication. If you think about it, God moving toward us, pursuing us as we approach Him, is the only way we can get in the face and presence of God.

Through prayer, we get in the face, in the presence, of our God.

Hopefully by now you're beginning to understand how much Jesus loves you and how much He desires a face-to-face, intimate sit-down with you. But I want to make sure you understand what I call the blessings of prayer. God uses our direct communication with Him to bless us and grow us in ways you probably haven't even fathomed. In the next chapter, we'll look closely at why God calls His people to talk with Him. But first, use the following reflection questions to help you examine your heart and your prayer life.

Let's Talk

- Is it hard for you to believe God is into you? Why or why not?
- Are you prone to sit-downs or drive-throughs with God?
- Have you ever felt like Peter did after he denied Jesus—ashamed and like you wanted to hide from God? How did you respond? Did you doubt that you were still loved and worthy of talking with God? Why or why not?
- Is anything keeping you from an intimate, face-to-face sit-down with Jesus? If so, what?

Chapter 2

THE TRANSFORMATION

Why Does God Call Us to Pray?

My sheep listen to my voice; I know them, and they follow me.
—John 10:27

I PROBABLY DON'T HAVE to tell you that we live in a day and time when we want—and even expect—answers *now*. Immediate gratification is the goal. If I want to eat Indian food, I can get on my phone, and it's at my door. If I need groceries, I can go online and in as little as an hour, I can have finished the grocery shopping for the week. If you need an oil change, you can pull up to the service station and in twenty minutes be on your way. The list of immediate conveniences at our disposal is endless.

When it comes to life issues, we find people running to everything for immediate answers—horoscopes, dating sites, psychics, tarot cards, life coaches, self-professed prophets—everything but God. Very few run to God to seek clarity and direction for their careers, relationships, and families.

If you don't have a prayer life, then you look for temporary relief in these kinds of things. If you don't have a prayer life, then you take whatever hand is extended, thinking that's your help. Without a prayer life that allows you to know God's voice, you jump on the next opportunity, believing it's from God. How many times have you leaped, thinking God had opened the door, only to realize He had so much more for you? If only you could have discerned His voice.

When we live a life of prayer, we recognize His voice, and He knows ours. As Jesus told the crowd of Pharisees in John's Gospel, "My sheep listen to my voice; I know them, and they follow me" (John 10:27).

CALLED TO PRAY

When I was in high school, I was taught how to talk to God (more about that in chapter 3). But it wasn't until I was a sophomore at Alabama State University in Montgomery that I felt *called* to pray. I was with college friends in the local Piggly Wiggly when an elderly woman named Mother Davis came into my life. Looking back now, I think God just plopped this old lady into our lives. There's just no other way to explain how the paths of young college students and someone like Mother Davis would intersect. Some might call it serendipitous; I just call it providential.

Mother Davis was a short, slender but strong woman with smooth dark skin. We struck up a conversation with her, and she ended up inviting us to her home (I know. It sounds crazy; that's why I know it was God). We quickly learned that Mother Davis was a praying woman. She didn't have a television and lived with very little. She would say, "My house is dedicated to nothing but prayer." She always knew that God would send her people for the purpose of teaching and calling them to pray.

Mother Davis was downright weird, but she taught me

so much. When we went to her house, we would have what we called "shut-ins." I remember the first night we had a shut-in. She locked the door and said, "OK, we're going to pray all night." My friends and I looked at each other and I thought, "This old woman has just locked us in her house." That night, we prayed for an hour, read the Bible for an hour, and then spent the rest of the night doing the same: praying, reading, praying, reading. Over the years, we built a special relationship with her. She told us, "God has sent me into your lives to teach you how to pray, to build up your prayer life." Mother Davis taught me how to pray for hours. She taught me how to start a conversation with God and that prayer is essential to a relationship with Him, as essential as water to life. She showed me that talking to Jesus is how I pursue Him—and how He pursues me.

> How many times have you leaped, thinking God had opened the door, only to realize He had so much more for you?

Back in our dorm rooms on campus, my friends and I were on fire for God. I'd say we brought the same radical prayers we learned at Mother Davis' house back to campus. We prayed so fervently, so loud, that the resident assistant would call security on us. He'd knock on the door and tell us to quiet down. But we didn't let that stop us and usually got ousted from our rooms. Then we'd walk to the football field and continue our prayer meeting. Sometimes we'd get in our cars and drive to parks in Montgomery and pray. At lunchtime on campus, we'd go to an area called "the yard," form a circle, and pray. Pretty soon, people were coming up, getting in the circle, and letting us pray for them. It was the first time God used me to call for corporate prayer. My nickname in college was "John the B" (for John the Baptist).

In many ways, I think of college as my island of Patmos, where John, one of Jesus' twelve disciples, was exiled. On that island, God gave John the vision for the new earth we read about in Revelation. During that time in college, I really got to know God through prayer. I was there to get a degree, but so much more happened to me. Like John did on that tiny Greek island, I began to really meet God in Alabama in such an intimate way. I spent so much time talking to Him in prayer that I started to really hear and know His voice.

I remember one time when His voice was almost audible to me. I watched young men who I knew were Christians come to college and, one by one, give in to the pressures of college life and leave their faith. I saw some even publicly renounce Jesus. I remember at one point going into my dorm room, closing the door, and falling to my knees. I just began to weep and cry out to God. I told Him that I never wanted to go back to who I used to be before I met Him. And I heard the Lord ask me a simple question, much like the one He asked Peter in John 21: "Do you love Me?"

The question just brought more tears. I said, "You know I love You." And He said to me in prayer, "As long as you love Me, you'll never go back to who you used to be. Stay with Me. Continue to build our relationship. I've already told you in My Word, 'I'll never leave you. I'll never forsake you. I am with you always.'" Did you get that? All of that happened in prayer. I really began to understand how prayer gives us a direct line to God and can powerfully change us.

The thing is, God calls *every* believer to pray. In prayer, we put our trust in Him and come into the family of God. After that, He wants to have direct communication with us, and He wants the relationship to grow and mature. But some believers don't answer that call. And they're missing out on true intimacy with the One who created and died for them. Please don't let that be you. Draw near to God, and He will draw near to you.

I want more than anything for your heart and mind to understand why God has called you to a life of prayer. There's a reason God commanded us to talk with Him, made a way for us to talk with Him, and gave us the perfect model of divine communication in Jesus. He has called us to a life of prayer to bring blessings into our lives—and to change us.

A Life of Prayer Transforms Us

In prayer, we are consistently on the wheel of the Potter. Have you ever thought about that? As we continue to talk with God, thus strengthening our relationship with Him, He's shaping and molding us into masterpieces that will ultimately be revealed in eternity. You don't have to look much further than the disciples to see how Jesus transforms His followers. Think about who the Twelve were before they met Jesus. We know that Andrew, James, John, and Peter were fishermen. Matthew was a tax collector. Simon may have been a politician.

Whatever their professions, who they were before they met Jesus is not who they were when He left them. They were changed. Peter went on to lead the church. Andrew went on to preach the gospel to the Scythians and Thracians. Bartholomew preached in India. James was a local missionary in Jerusalem. How they died is also telling. All but John and Judas are believed to have been crucified, stoned, or otherwise martyred for preaching and telling others about Jesus. I don't know about you, but I can't think of anything that says "transformed" better than that.

> I want more than anything for your heart and mind to understand why God has called you to a life of prayer.

But catch this, because this is good: Jesus spent 80 percent of His time with these men He handpicked to journey with—communicating with them, listening to them, talking with them, walking with them, fellowshipping with them. That relationship was the change catalyst. Someone once told me, "You'll be able to see what you've prayed five years from now." Your life will reflect your communication. The disciples' lives, after the resurrection and ascension, reflected their communication with Jesus. They were transformed.

My mom died of cancer when I was in my thirties. The whole time she was sick, I prayed and prayed for God to heal her, but He did not give me what I wanted. Looking back, I see that He used my mom's death—and the time leading up to it—in so many ways, especially in my sister's life. Through that experience, He conditioned me to lead. I knew I would have to step up to be the leader of the family and adopt my sister, who was twelve or thirteen at the time. Not only was I dealing with my mom's death; I was also walking through the repositioning that had to happen. My wife and I had to seek wisdom to raise a teenage girl. I was now praying for her *and* for unity in our home.

Your thirties is early to lose your mom, especially when there's no other parent in the picture. I felt like God had cheated me. But it took me talking with God to understand that He had to take my mom for me to get my sister. My sister would not be the woman she is today had she not come to live with my wife and me. Unbeknownst to me, she was off the tracks. I had no idea what I was bringing into my home. It was rough! I was trying to do ministry and build a strong marriage, all while still grieving for my mom, and then I had to deal with a teenager's antics. But I see the finished product now. My sister is a minister and married with three beautiful children. She's amazing. I'm blown away by her, but she is not who we received twenty-plus years ago. Prayer transformed all three of us. Bottom line: if God doesn't change the situation, then in prayer He conditions us to go through the situation.

Prayer Builds Our Trust

When we cultivate a life of prayer, trust and relationship are built as we begin to hear God's voice. As we regularly communicate with Him through prayer, we start to see His nature and witness firsthand that the God we talk to, worship, and serve is a God who keeps His promises. In many ways, we can see how communication builds trust in our human relationships.

When Anna and I first met, I realized pretty quickly that she had trust issues with men. As we began to talk each day, the relationship grew and so did the trust between us. The more we communicated, the more comfortable Anna felt. And the more she began to trust that I would keep my promises to take care of our family. As we talked and were present with each other, Anna came to know me as someone who had her best interests in mind. Today she'll tell you she's never had to worry about whether the lights were going to come on when she hit the switch. She's never had to ask if the mortgage had been paid. She doesn't have to worry about me cheating. She doesn't worry about those things because of the relationship and trust we've built through open lines of communication.

> If God doesn't change the situation, then in prayer He conditions us to go through the situation.

Through daily prayer, we get to know God, and as we do, we learn that we can trust Him to keep His word. Trust makes us more secure in our relationship with Him and confident that He is walking with us, that He is present with us. He gives us direction and meets our needs. Our role is simply to talk with Him, listen to His voice, and follow His instructions.

This reminds me of one of the most powerful examples of trust in Scripture. In 2 Kings 4, we meet a woman whose husband has recently died. Verse 1 tells us her husband followed God, even serving in the company of the prophets. It makes sense that she would go to Elisha and cry out in desperation, "Your servant my husband is dead, and you know that he revered the LORD. But now his creditor is coming to take my two boys as his slaves" (v. 1).

Elisha asked her, "How can I help you? Tell me, what do you have in your house?"

She said, "Your servant has nothing there at all...except a small jar of olive oil" (v. 2).

She had "a little oil." Now the ball was in her court. Would this widow trust Elisha and do what Elisha told her to do, as crazy as it sounded? Let's read the story:

> Elisha said, "Go around and ask all your neighbors for empty jars. Don't ask for just a few. Then go inside and shut the door behind you and your sons. Pour oil into all the jars, and as each is filled, put it to one side." She left him and shut the door behind her and her sons. They brought the jars to her and she kept pouring. When all the jars were full, she said to her son, "Bring me another one." But he replied, "There is not a jar left." Then the oil stopped flowing.
>
> She went and told the man of God, and he said, "Go, sell the oil and pay your debts. You and your sons can live on what is left."
>
> —2 Kings 4:3–7

A lifetime of prayer built trust. Because she knew Elisha was a man of God, she trusted he would help her. She recognized the voice of God and acted in obedience. A life of prayer led her to call on Elisha and trust his words when the darkest hours came.

We have this promise. The longer you experience relationship with God, the more trust you'll have that He'll meet your needs and He's there walking with you and strengthening you to stand firm in unshakable faith.

Prayer Brings Rest

In this world of so much unrest, I'm so thankful that in prayer, I can rest in Jesus. He is my high tower. In the Old Testament, towers were used as fortresses in times of war. Let's look at what Judges 9:51 says: "But there was a strong tower in the city, and all the men and women—all the people of the city—fled there and shut themselves in; then they went up to the top of the tower" (NKJV). Nineteenth-century Bible scholar George Bush explains that the high tower was seen as a large "retreat."

> Doubtless a sort of citadel such as exists in most considerable towns in western Asia, and which serves the people as a last retreat when the town is taken by an enemy, and where the people shut themselves up on occasions of popular tumult.[1]

I love that comparison. It's comforting to know that when the world is shaking under our feet, we can run to our "high tower" and rest in Him. How do we run to Him? In prayer.

Scripture also tells us Christ is our secret place: "He that dwelleth in the secret place of the most High shall abide under the shadow of the Almighty" (Ps. 91:1, KJV). To dwell means to live there. Through a life of prayer, we can "abide under the shadow of the Almighty." That's a powerful place to be. You can rest in that place.

Building our new church is one of the most difficult things I've done. Throughout the construction process, I've felt a lot like the Israelites, who had so many obstacles standing in the way of them entering the Promised Land. It's been like that with this project. I was telling one of my mentors, Apostle I. V. Hilliard, about all the challenges we've been facing, and he said, "Every delay will be to your benefit."

> When the world is shaking under your feet, you can run to your "high tower" and rest in Him.

Basically, he was telling me, "In all of this, rest in knowing that God has you." In the midst of us developing the campus, the completion date has been pushed multiple times. At one point, I was told the facility would be ready in time for Easter services. Again, it wasn't complete—but to God be the glory! On Easter weekend 2020, every church was closed. Had that building been ready, we would've been paying a mortgage on a building we couldn't even open. It's true. Every delay has been to our benefit. In other words, rest in the prayers; rest in the time; rest in the relationship, knowing what Romans 8:28 promises us: all things are going to work together for your good.

You don't get to this place of rest and peace without communication, without prayer. I love the first two verses of David's Psalm 62: "Truly my soul finds rest in God; my salvation comes from him. Truly he is my rock and my salvation; he is my fortress, I will never be shaken."

Prayer Can Change God's Mind!

By now, my guess is you know that I'm not one to make a claim unless I can prove it with Scripture. Unless it's in the Bible, you won't hear me saying some story or church doctrine is truth. I fully believe Scripture—that God's Word is a lamp unto our feet. So trust me. I wouldn't make a claim as audacious as prayer being able to change God's mind if it wasn't grounded in Scripture.

We can actually find several examples of how prayer changed God's intention in the Bible. When Moses was on Mount Sinai and the Israelites built a golden calf, God was ready to destroy all of them. He called them "stiff-necked people" and told Moses, "Now leave me alone so that my anger may burn against them and that I may destroy them" (Exod. 32:10). Do you get what's happening here? God is getting ready to send down fire. He's getting ready to obliterate them. But Moses prayed, throwing himself on the Lord's mercy. He got between God and the people, thinking fast to make his argument. And it was a good one. He pointed out what God had already done to rescue His people:

> But Moses sought the favor of the LORD his God. "LORD," he said, "why should your anger burn against your people, whom you brought out of Egypt with great power and a mighty hand? Why should the Egyptians say, 'It was with evil intent that he brought them out, to kill them in the mountains and to wipe them off the face of the earth'? Turn from your fierce anger; relent and do not bring disaster on your people."
>
> —EXODUS 32:11–12

And God relented.

Another time, God was ready to destroy the whole city of Nineveh (a metroplex so large that it took three days to go through). But the people called "urgently" to God, repented, and prayed for mercy (Jon. 3:8). "When God saw what they did and how they turned from their evil ways, he relented and did not bring on them the destruction he had threatened" (Jon. 3:10).

Notice that the examples we see in Scripture are of God changing His mind about punishment as a result of prayer. We don't see Him promising to do something good and then changing His mind. The author and finisher of our faith doesn't break His promises.

Why does God call us to spend our lives talking with Him? Hopefully, you're beginning to understand how prayer tethers us. Think about the movies or news footage you've seen of astronauts doing spacewalks outside the spaceship. They use safety ropes that hook one end to the spacewalker and the other to the vehicle.[2] If for any reason the line becomes disconnected, the astronaut could be lost and left floating in space. Prayer is like the astronaut's safety tether. It's our lifeline.

That's why learning how to talk to God is so important. But my guess is before you learn how to communicate with Him, you still need to be convinced that you need to be *taught* to pray. Maybe you're even insulted by that thought. After all, prayer is just talking with God, right? That's not rocket science. You just open your mouth and speak. I get it. It would be like someone coming in and saying, "I need to teach you how to walk." I can hear the response: "Are you crazy? I've been walking since I was one. I don't need to learn how to walk. I've been doing it all my life. Go sell crazy somewhere else!"

You've probably been praying for years, maybe decades. But I'm asking you to trust me and move ahead with me in this journey. It's one I believe will build in you a faith that will not be shaken.

LET'S TALK

- When was the last time you recognized God's voice in your life?
- Do you sense that God recognizes your voice? Why or why not?
- When you think about being on the Potter's wheel, what comes to mind? Is it a picture you welcome or one that is difficult for you to imagine? Please explain your answer (and be honest).
- Do you believe prayer has ever changed you or a situation you were facing? Why or why not?
- Have you ever experienced God as your "high tower" and place of rest? Please explain your answer.
- Why is talking to God so critical to you building trust in God? (Please be specific.)

Chapter 3

TO SEEK HIS FACE

Why Do We Need to Be Taught to Pray?

One day Jesus was praying in a certain place. When he finished, one of his disciples said to him, "Lord, teach us to pray, just as John taught his disciples."
—LUKE 11:1

SO MANY TIMES, they had seen Him leave the crowd or their group and separate Himself. They had heard Him praying by Himself and in their midst. They had watched Him open His hands, look up, and give thanks. And they had seen the results of their Master's prayers.

So it made sense that after watching and hearing Him pray one day, the twelve men He had chosen to mentor said to Jesus, "Master, teach us how to pray." The disciples were around prayer; they saw Jesus go off to spend time with the Father. They desired to do what Jesus did and have what He had. I can imagine them telling Jesus: "Every time You come back, You return amazing. Every time You come back, You bring revelation. You have wisdom for life. What are You doing? You call us friends. You say, 'You didn't choose Me; I chose you.' So if You chose us, choose us to also know how to have what You have. Teach us what we've seen and heard You do."

Notice that Jesus didn't say to them, "You already know how to pray," or, "Just speak to the Father; He knows your heart." No, Jesus looked at them and gave them the words that many of us grew up learning and are still repeated in our worship today—words that have been proclaimed from pulpits, whispered in combat, and put to music.

> Our Father which art in heaven, Hallowed be thy name. Thy kingdom come, Thy will be done in earth, as it is in heaven. Give us this day our daily bread. And forgive us our debts, as we forgive our debtors. And lead us not into temptation, but deliver us from evil: For thine is the kingdom, and the power, and the glory, for ever. Amen.
>
> —MATTHEW 6:9–13, KJV

Jesus wasn't saying, "Every time you pray, speak these words." He was giving them a template, a *way* to pray. Scripture tells us that we were born into sin and shaped in iniquity (Ps. 51:5). We're spiritually dead. But when we put our faith in Christ and become believers, we learn this new communication. Prayer is two-way, direct conversation that builds relationship. Jesus knows we need to be taught this new way of communication with our heavenly Father. It's almost like learning a second language with a new vocabulary and specific criteria for using certain words.

Running to the Father

I remember the first time a gentleman named Edward Christian told me and seventeen other young men in my church, "I want to teach you to pray." As I mentioned earlier, my father was not in my life in the way he should have been. There are three men whose thumbprints are on my life, and the first man to spiritually mentor me was Edward. He grabbed me at a time when I could've gone a different direction. When I was seventeen, he handed me my first Bible, *The Open Bible*. I took it to college with me. I still have it. The pages are falling out, and almost every page is marked up.

Edward instilled in me a love for the Word of God. He also bought me my first Bible commentary and taught me how to research, study, and memorize Scripture. He kept up with me throughout my college years at Alabama State, regularly calling and checking in on me. Every time I came home from college, he would pick me up and pray with me. Looking back, I realize it was amazing how God placed him in my life. Edward left an indelible mark on my life.

But it all started with the Bible study he led. We called ourselves the Timothy Club. Every Thursday, we'd all gather in the basement of our church to study Scripture and pray together. Every Sunday morning after church services, they would set up rows of tables in a basement room, where the whole church would eat lunch together. But during the week, we could use that room for whatever we needed. I like to call it the Cave because when David ran into the Cave of Adullam to seek refuge from King Saul, four hundred men followed, and those same men became David's mighty men of valor. They were trained in the cave. (You can read about it in 1 Samuel 22.)

In much the same way, Edward Christian showed us how to be young men of God down in our church's cave. We sat at the tables with our Bibles open and our notebooks, pens, and highlighters ready. Out of those seventeen boys, fifteen of us, including me, became preachers. One of them goes to our church. Edward died of sickle cell anemia at a young age, but his son is also a member of our church. His legacy continues.

I grew up hearing my grandmother pray, but when Edward said he wanted to teach us a new communication, I knew he was about to teach me how to go to God on my own—just as the disciples knew what Jesus was about to do for them when He agreed to teach them to pray. I had been around Edward, listening to him pray and seeing the results of his prayers, and I wanted what he had. Until that time in my life, I had always gone to Edward, asking him, "Please pray for this for me."

Edward knew he had to point us in the direction of God. He knew he wouldn't always be in our lives. We were babes in Christ, but Edward Christian was about to teach us to crawl on our own, to walk on our own, to eat on our own. He was going to teach us to communicate with God, our Father, without his involvement and make us totally dependent on God, not him. I will always be thankful to Edward. He gave us such a gift.

I think about Samuel when he was a kid looking after the aging priest, Eli. God was calling Samuel's name, but he didn't understand and he continued to go to Eli, thinking Eli was the one calling him. The third time Samuel went to him, Eli knew what was happening:

> A third time the LORD called, "Samuel!" And Samuel got up and went to Eli and said, "Here I am; you called me." Then Eli realized that the LORD was calling the boy. So Eli told Samuel, "Go and lie down, and if he calls you, say, 'Speak, LORD, for your servant is listening.'"
>
> —1 SAMUEL 3:8–9

What was Eli doing? He was teaching Samuel how to pray and build a relationship through open communication, because before then Samuel had been running to Eli. We've been taught to run to our parents or our pastor. The disciples were used to running to Jesus. I was used to running to Edward. But that's not what Jesus died for. He sacrificed Himself on the cross so that we could have direct communication and relationship with our Savior. When Jesus taught His disciples to pray, He was pointing them in the right direction—toward a relationship with the Father.

WHAT PRAYER ISN'T

Edward also showed us that prayer wasn't going to God only when we wanted or needed something. I grew up hearing people talk about prayer like that. Anytime someone would mention a need or say, "I'm going through a really hard time right now," before they could get the words out of their mouths, someone within earshot was saying, "Well, did you pray about that? Did you ask God to heal you?"

Yes, we can take our wants and needs to God. Absolutely, we can ask for healing, for reconciliation, for protection, for comfort, for provision, for a relationship. First Peter 5:7 tells us, "Cast all your anxiety on him because he cares for you." But prayer is so much more than listing our needs. God is so much more than a magic genie or Santa Claus. Prayer is so much more than what you do when your back is against the wall. Remember this: *We talk to God to seek His face, not His hand.* When you're face to face with someone you love, you're not thinking about what they can do for you or what you need. It's the same with Jesus. When you're seeking the face of God like we talked about in chapter 1, you're seeking to know Him, to be in relationship with Him, to look into His eyes.

I've had those people in my life who see me as someone they can leverage or use for their own benefit. Every time we're together, I know they're going to ask something of me. My guess is you've had people like that in your life too. I don't know about you, but I avoid those people. I'm pretty much always busy when they call. God isn't looking for people who only seek His hand. He's looking for hearts that seek *Him*. He wants for us what He had with Moses, Samuel, and Peter, for us to walk with Him and talk with Him.

> We talk to God to seek His face, not His hand.

But it's up to you. God has invited you to walk hand in hand and face to face with Him. He has promised us that when we call out to Him, He hears us. First Peter 3:12 tells us that God's ears are "attentive" to our prayers. And when we come to Him, we can even come with *His* words. Have you ever thought about that? Sometimes when I just don't have the words to say, I go to Scripture and let God's Word form my prayers. When we pray His Word, we pray the truth. The Bible promises us that His Word will not return void, that it must accomplish what it is sent to do.

> So is my word that goes out from my mouth: It will not return to me empty, but will accomplish what I desire and achieve the purpose for which I sent it.
>
> —Isaiah 55:11

In prayer, we can quote Scripture and even remind God and ourselves of what He has said. There's nothing more powerful. I've always loved that when Jesus was tempted in the wilderness for forty days after being baptized and filled with the Holy Spirit, He just pounded Satan with Scripture. Every time Satan said something to test Him, Jesus had an "it is written" comeback from the Word of His Father. It was an epic smackdown. When Satan commanded Him to turn stones into bread, Jesus said, "It is written, 'Man shall not live by bread alone'" (Luke 4:4, ESV). When Satan offered Him control of all kingdoms if He'd worship him, Jesus said, "It is written, 'You shall worship the Lord your God, and him only shall you serve'" (Luke 4:8, ESV). Stop and take a minute to read the whole passage in Luke 4:1–13. You'll love it.

A New Way to Pray

It's a harsh reality, but some people don't go to God because they're lazy. Yet far more of us don't go to Him because we don't know how. In part 2, I'm going to share how Edward Christian taught me to pray. Edward told our group, "If you study the Lord's Prayer, you'll see why Jesus gave the disciples those words. He was giving them a format." Edward called it ACTSI (adoration, confession, thankfulness, supplication, intercession). He gave us a paper with those words on it and told us to keep it in our Bibles. He taught us what each term meant and then said, "It's up to you to take this and use it to go to God on your own and seek His face."

I realize now that the ACTSI mnemonic tool isn't original to Edward. A lot of people use and teach it (though I've yet to see others add the *I* for intercession). But it was new to me when I was seventeen, and I've never forgotten how it changed the way I talked with God. It's what I began teaching thirty years ago, and it's what I teach now. This training transformed my relationship with God and gave me life.

When Edward taught me to pray, I wanted to pray more. And that's what I want for you. I want to cultivate a desire in you to pray. I hope learning how to talk with God compels you to want to talk with Him more and leads you to a life of prayer and unshakable faith. That's actually my prayer for you! When I began to talk with God the ACTSI way, I began to see Him and prayer differently. So let's move to part 2 of the book to discover how each discipline in the ACTSI tool gives us a new way of talking to God—and, in the process, changes our hearts.

LET'S TALK

- Do you think you need to be taught to pray? Why or why not?
- How would you like to see your prayer life and relationship with Jesus change?

- Why do you think Jesus taught the disciples the Lord's Prayer?
- Have you fallen into the trap of turning God into a magic genie? Do you think this is easy to do? Why or why not?
- Do you find yourself wanting to pray often? (Be honest.)

PART II
ACTSI
(ADORATION, CONFESSION, THANKSGIVING, SUPPLICATION, INTERCESSION)

Chapter 4

NOTHING BUT PRAISE

How Does Adoration Bring God Near?

O God, God of our ancestors, are you not God in heaven above and ruler of all kingdoms below?
—2 Chronicles 20:6, msg

The Moabites, Ammonites, and Meunites had made an alliance. They'd come together to collectively defeat their enemy, Jehoshaphat, the king of Judah. Before long, Jehoshaphat received an intelligence report saying the armies were on their way to him and had already made it halfway to Judah. The king was visibly shaken. But instead of assembling his best war strategists in a room to build a military plan, Jehoshaphat went to God for help and ordered a nationwide fast.

The whole country united in prayer to seek the Lord's help. It was then that we see a powerful display of adoration and praise. In front of all the people who had assembled in the courtyard of the temple of God—fathers, mothers, children—Jehoshaphat praised and honored God. Let's read the story in *The Message*.

> O God, God of our ancestors, are you not God in heaven above and ruler of all kingdoms below? You hold all power and might in your fist—no one

> stands a chance against you! And didn't you make the natives of this land leave as you brought your people Israel in, turning it over permanently to your people Israel, the descendants of Abraham your friend? They have lived here and built a holy house of worship to honor you, saying, "When the worst happens—whether war or flood or disease or famine—and we take our place before this Temple (we know you are personally present in this place!) and pray out our pain and trouble, we know that you will listen and give victory."
>
> —2 CHRONICLES 20:5–9

Look at how Jehoshaphat built God up, praising Him for His nature: "God in heaven…ruler of all kingdoms…. You hold all power and might in your fist—no one stands a chance against you!" Through his adoration, Jehoshaphat got God's attention.

In Matthew 20, we see another less-wordy display of adoration, but it's no less compelling. As Jesus was making His way to Jerusalem, He met two blind men outside of Jericho. We don't know if they had been blind from birth. But we can be sure these men knew what it felt like to be outcasts from society—to wonder if they'd eat that day because someone had pity on them or if apathy and cynicism would send them to bed hungry. When they heard Jesus was passing by, they cried out, "Have mercy on us, Son of David."

Jehoshaphat and the two blind men always remind me of what gets God's attention. Our God is used to being honored and adored. Our petition or need, even when the need is severe, doesn't get His attention. He's not used to being surrounded by complaints, murmuring, and orders like, "Give me; give me; give me. Do this for me." The Alpha and Omega first responds to adoration.

Our God is used to being honored and adored. Our petition or need, even when the need is severe, doesn't get His attention.

Let's go back to the Lord's Prayer. Look at the first line: "Our Father in heaven, hallowed be Your name" (Matt. 6:9, NKJV). This is adoration, and it sets the tone for the rest of the words Jesus gives His disciples when they ask Him to teach them how to pray. Adoration is how it all starts. The word *adoration* comes from the Latin *adōrātiō*, which means "to give homage or worship to someone or something."[1] When we adore Him, we look up and acknowledge God for who He is—His very nature.

How Will You Label God?

Think about David, who began most of his psalms in adoration and praise. David messed up more times than we know. His sins were many, including murder. But even though David coveted his neighbor's wife, Bathsheba, slept with her, schemed for her husband's death when she told David she was pregnant with his child, and had Uriah murdered (that's a long, running list of sins), God described him as "a man after My own heart" (Acts 13:22, NKJV). David was a worshipper. He took time to honor and adore God. He spoke well of Him, and I can't help but think God loved to hear what David would say. He may have looked at David and thought, "How are you going to label Me today? Am I going to be Father, Lord, Master? Am I going to be the high tower? The apple of your eye? Choir director? How will you praise Me today?"

Throughout Scripture, we see God's people coming to Him with worshipful words: Lord, Master, Father, God. In fact, most of the time, the men and women we read about in the Old and New Testaments began their prayers by identifying who God is and declaring His nature. Let's look at a few examples:

> You alone are the LORD. You made the heavens, even the highest heavens, and all their starry host, the earth and all that is on it, the seas and all that is in them. You give life to everything, and the multitudes of heaven worship you.
>
> —NEHEMIAH 9:6

> For the LORD your God is God in heaven above and on the earth below.
>
> —JOSHUA 2:11

> For the director of music. According to gittith. A psalm of David. LORD, our Lord, how majestic is your name in all the earth! You have set your glory in the heavens.
>
> —PSALM 8:1

> How great are his signs, how mighty his wonders! His kingdom is an eternal kingdom; his dominion endures from generation to generation.
>
> —DANIEL 4:3

> Day and night they never stop saying: "'Holy, holy, holy is the Lord God Almighty,' who was, and is, and is to come."
>
> —REVELATION 4:8

> "Blessed is the king who comes in the name of the Lord!" "Peace in heaven and glory in the highest!"
>
> —Luke 19:38

> Praise be to the God and Father of our Lord Jesus Christ, who has blessed us in the heavenly realms with every spiritual blessing in Christ.
>
> —Ephesians 1:3

> We have only one God, and he is the Father. He created everything, and we live for him. Jesus Christ is our only Lord. Everything was made by him, and by him life was given to us.
>
> —1 Corinthians 8:6, CEV

Ushering In His Presence

When we begin our prayers by honoring, praising, and adoring God, we put Him in His rightful place, and we acknowledge our place beneath Him. In a sense, we roll out the red carpet for Him. Adoration gets God's attention and prepares our hearts. It also brings God close to us.

Years ago, I preached a sermon about how through praise, we invite God to come and join us in our times of prayer. I put a chair on the stage and tied a rope to one of the chair legs and then tossed the rope into the audience. I told the crowd, "Every time you say a word of adoration, pull the rope." Each time they shouted a word, they pulled the rope and the chair moved closer to them.

"You see, when you begin to adore God," I said, "you pull the throne in your direction." Psalm 22:3 says that He inhabits, or is "enthroned in," the praises of Israel (NKJV). God *sits* in the praises of His people. When we continuously adore Him, He moves in our direction because He appreciates it when we build Him up, when He's surrounded by adoration—because that's what He's used to.

> When we begin our prayers by honoring…God, we put Him in His rightful place…we roll out the red carpet for Him.

Look at the scene in Revelation 4:10–11. When John is whisked to heaven and told to write down everything he sees, he describes the vision God gives him: "The twenty-four elders fall down before the One seated on the throne, and they worship Him who lives forever and ever. They cast their crowns before the throne, saying: 'Worthy are You, our Lord and God, to receive glory and honor and power, for You created all things; by Your will they exist and came to be'" (BSB).

For us, adoration is almost like building God a place to sit. Think about the altars of the Old Testament. God's people built altars to Him as a form of adoration. When God told Abraham His plans to multiply Abraham's descendants and give them the Promised Land, Abraham immediately built an altar to praise Him. Alone on the mountain with God, Moses wrote down the Ten Commandments and got up early to build an altar (Exod. 24:4).

After the ark was on dry land, Noah built an altar to God, sacrificing one of every clean animal and bird on it (Gen. 8:20). Look what happened: "The Lord smelled the soothing aroma; and the Lord said to Himself, 'I will never again curse the ground on account of man, for the intent of man's heart is evil from his youth; and I will never again destroy every living thing, as I have done'"

(Gen. 8:21, NASB). In adoration, we tell God, "Before I share what I'm going through, let me build You a seat. Let me give You what You're used to. Let me surround You with praise."

All on Him

Starting our prayers with adoration also causes us to turn to Him and keep our eyes, ears, and words focused on Him. We're not thinking about everything that's going on in our lives and everything we want to tell Him. We're not remembering that fight with our spouse the other day or how hurt we were when that friend betrayed us or the terrible meeting with our boss. We're not even thinking about the brokenness of this world. We're just focusing on our Creator and Savior, honoring Him—in the same way He was extolled more than two thousand years ago and is continuously praised in heaven today.

> Adoration causes us to turn to Him and keep our eyes, ears, and words focused on Him.

Our thoughts and our attention are *all* on Him. The first half hour of my prayer time is nothing but adoration. Often, if not all the time, I get so caught up with praising Him that I lose track of time. Many times, I'm brought to tears thinking about how worthy He is to be praised. I love the chorus of "Revelation Song" because the lyrics echo the praise that continuously surrounds Him in heaven: "'Holy, holy, holy is the Lord God Almighty,' who was, and is, and is to come" (Rev. 4:8).

What I've realized through the years is the more I adore Him and acknowledge how big He is, the smaller my problems and myself become. As I focus on Him, He lifts the weight—of ministry, of leadership, of relationships, of just…life. The more I adore Him, the more He turns my mourning into joy. No longer am I wasting time and energy thinking about what happened the other day in the leadership meeting or the conversation I had yesterday with someone upset about something that happened in church. When you start with adoration, your thoughts shift from your burden or trial to Christ and His work on the cross. Your thoughts, your words—they're *all* focused on Him.

Building Your Vocabulary of Praise

I still remember a midnight prayer meeting I helped lead. The prayer conference organizers didn't expect fifteen thousand people to show up at midnight, but there they were all in one room—and the conference leaders weren't prepared. So I asked for words of adoration to be projected on the screen throughout the night to build up an atmosphere of worship. I had previously led a prayer conference at our church that drew sixteen thousand people, and during that event I'd made a list of seventy-five words of adoration. I explained how to pray using the ACTSI tool, and as we talked about adoration, I told the crowd, "We're going to say together the words that come across the screen. Just keep repeating the words you see up there."

Imagine fifteen thousand people calling out words and phrases of adoration. Praise filled the room—the power was almost palpable! It was so beautiful to see fifteen thousand people with their heads raised, arms lifted, and hands outstretched just praising God, ushering in His presence, and shifting their thoughts as the rest of the world faded away and their spirits were renewed. We were truly one body, one mind, one heart. It was a foretaste of heaven.

Wherever you are right now, take a minute to stop and declare the words that follow. (I've also included this list as Appendix A to make the words easy to find.) Say, "Jesus, You are…" before each word or phrase, and focus on Him and how worthy He is.

wonderful
mighty
amazing
good
magnificent
glorious
the Prince of Peace
great
strong
my defender
my champion
like no other
my counselor
my closest friend
my Abba Father

the center of my joy
my deliverer
my healer
my foundation
the air I breathe
my peace
my joy
the smile on my face
the beat of my heart
the skip in my step
all I have
all I want
all I need
Emmanuel
Jehovah Jireh, the Lord my provider

Jehovah Rapha, the Lord my healer

my protector

my hero

my superman

my hiding place

my counselor

my refuge

the alert God

the aware God

the God who never slumbers

all wise

my respite

my Father

my all in all

my cornerstone

my Messiah

sovereign in all Your ways

the God who reigns

all-powerful

the lover of my soul

my portion

my rock

my high tower

my redeemer

my waymaker

I believe adoration builds your vocabulary of praise. If we know that adoration gets the Lord's attention, then don't we want to find and say words that turn the throne toward us, that bring His kingdom to earth, compelling Him to dwell in our midst? There's no end to the attributes you can declare about God: holy, mighty, great, wonderful, excellent, magnificent. There's also, "Victorious God, the God who fights for me, the God who always wins—You're my peace; You're my joy; You're the beat of my heart; You're the reason I get up." And then there are the words that describe how God has personally moved in your life in specific situations and trials. All of that is just too much for Him to ignore.

After we spend time adoring and honoring God for who He is, we're ready to move on to the *C* in ACTSI: confession. Once we've ushered in God's presence, it's time to do what I call "clearing the room" and eliminate anything that may be blocking your communication with God. Get ready! Adoration is about bringing God near and building Him up; confession is about breaking you down, because if you don't clear the room, you can't expect God to stay.

Let's Talk

- How have you adored God in the past in your prayers? How can you spend more time in adoration?
- When was the last time you were able to fully focus on God in your prayers?
- Think about a time when you were so caught up in worship that the world seemed far away and you could feel the presence of the Holy Spirit. What led you into that place?
- What can you do to build up your praise vocabulary?
- Look at the list of words of adoration in this chapter or Appendix A and think about your life. Add specific words to the list that describe how Christ has touched your life and use them in your prayers.

Chapter 5

CLEARING THE ROOM

Why Is Confession So Essential in Prayer?

Against you, you only, have I sinned and done
what is evil in your sight.
—Psalm 51:4

There he was, standing in front of David—his friend, trusted adviser, and God's messenger. Why had he come? What did Nathan the prophet have to say to him? Would this be the day of reckoning? Would all be revealed and so much darkness come to light?

Nathan had come to tell his shepherd-turned-king a story. It was a tale about two men, one rich and one poor. The rich man had many sheep and cattle. The poor one had only a lamb he loved dearly. It was like a child to him. A traveler came to the rich man but instead of killing one of his own sheep to prepare a meal for the traveler, the wealthy master took the poor man's only lamb.

David was outraged. The Bible says he "burned with anger": "As surely as the Lord lives, the man who did this must die!" he told Nathan. "He must pay for that lamb four times over, because he did such a thing and had no pity" (2 Sam. 12:5–6).

And then Nathan dropped the hammer, telling David, "*You* are the man" (2 Sam. 12:7, emphasis added).

Everything was in the light. The secret David had carried for almost a year was now disclosed. Without hesitation, David falls to his knees and confesses: "Then David said to Nathan, 'I have sinned against the LORD'" (2 Sam. 12:13).

We can learn a lot about confession from David. He takes ownership, full responsibility, for his sin. He makes no excuses. There's no finger-pointing or blaming others. No rationalization. No denial. No anger. David didn't know what God would do, but he knew it was possible he could die that day. In Psalm 51, David confesses and laments his sin, and we get this honest and beautiful assemblage of words as King David throws himself on God's mercy. Notice how he reminds God of His nature and unconditional love.

> Have mercy on me, O God, according to your unfailing love; according to your great compassion blot out my transgressions. Wash away all my iniquity and cleanse me from my sin. For I know my transgressions, and my sin is always before me. Against you, you only, have I sinned and done what is evil in your sight; so you are right in your verdict and justified when you judge.
>
> —PSALM 51:1–4

God calls us to confess in prayer because He doesn't want anything between us and Him. Our sin separates us from God. It blocks our communication with Him and puts static on the line.

Without confession, we don't have relationship. It's almost as if somebody has wronged you, but they never apologize, and then they come to you asking for help. I can tell you what I'd want to say: "*Whaaat*? You need something from me? But you never apologized for what you did to me. How can I even listen to your request?"

Without confession, we open the door for our adversary (the definition of the Hebrew word for Satan) to remind us of our shame, cause us to dwell on past sins that have been forgiven, and torment us over the sin we aren't sharing. The Bible calls Satan "our accuser" (Rev. 12:10). He brings up accusations, seeking to destroy you. I think about Judas when he betrayed Jesus and how he let Satan make fatal accusations. The moment Judas kissed Jesus on the cheek, Judas fled the Garden of Gethsemane, racked with guilt. He gave the enemy enough time to manipulate him spiritually and emotionally and bring up the charges.

Trust me, you don't want Satan revealing your sin to you; he'll deftly use it against you to keep you from your Redeemer. He'll use it to bring guilt and shame. You want to confess your sin to the Savior who died for you, who loves you unconditionally. Without confession, we "sit" in our sin. Another psalm from David reveals this truth. I think we tend to think that until Nathan confronted David, the king of Israel was content and at peace in his palace. After all, he had brought Bathsheba into his house after he had sent Uriah to the front lines to be killed in the war.

But in Psalm 32, David reveals what this hidden sin was doing to him: "When I kept silent about my sin, my body wasted away through my groaning all day long. For day and night Your hand was heavy upon me; my vitality failed as with the dry heat of summer" (vv. 3–5, NASB). David was racked with guilt. He couldn't sleep; he was losing weight.

He was miserable. Satan had him right where he wanted him, unable to accomplish the plans God had for his life.

> Without confession, you open the door for your adversary to rack you with guilt and interfere with the plans God has for your life.

We can be assured that God does not ignore our sin even when we don't confess. While He may delay judgment or the consequences of sin, He will never *ignore* it. He is crystal clear about that in His Word. In addition to David's testimony, we can consider Moses' example. As he commanded the Israelites to follow God's directions into battle, he told them that God knew their sin: "But if you fail to do this, you will be sinning against the LORD; and you may be sure that your sin will find you out" (Num. 32:23). Unconfessed sin makes us miserable, and it always comes to light. But because God is holy, He can't ignore our unconfessed sin, and He gives us an opportunity to return to Him. Just look at what happened when David confessed.

THE POWER OF CONFESSION

While confession is never easy, God calls us to confess, knowing it brings freedom and release. After David confessed his sin against God, this big, life-sucking weight bearing down on his shoulders like an anvil was lifted. He broke out of Satan's shackles and was able to move forward with God. Confession brings us to God in a way we never expected. Look at what Scripture tells us about the power of confession in our prayers. (All emphasis in the following scriptures has been added.)

- **We are forgiven and cleansed:** "If we confess our sins, he is faithful and just and will *forgive us our sins and purify us* from all unrighteousness" (1 John 1:9).
- **We receive mercy:** "Whoever conceals their sins does not prosper, but the one who confesses and renounces them *finds mercy*" (Prov. 28:13).
- **We are refreshed:** "Repent, then, and turn to God, so that your sins may be wiped out, that *times of refreshing* may come from the Lord" (Acts 3:19).
- **God remembers His covenant with us:** "But if they will confess their sins and the sins of their ancestors—their unfaithfulness and their hostility toward me…*I will remember my covenant* with Jacob and my covenant with Isaac and my covenant with Abraham, and I will remember the land" (Lev. 26:40–42).
- **We have salvation:** "Godly sorrow brings *repentance that leads to salvation* and leaves no regret, but worldly sorrow brings death" (2 Cor. 7:10).
- **We are heard:** "If my people, who are called by my name, will humble themselves and pray and seek my face and turn from their wicked ways, then *I will hear from heaven*, and I will forgive their sin and will heal their land" (2 Chron. 7:14).

I love that last scripture! When we confess and repent, God hears us from heaven. *Whoa!* Let that sink in. When we confess our sins, we clear the room. Through confession, you destroy all the evidence your enemy can use against you to try and block your communication with God and stifle your relationship with Him and His plans for your life. But I'm here to tell you that you won't get there until you go to an uncomfortable place of brokenness.

A BROKEN PLACE

Make no mistake. Confession isn't simply mindless rhetoric. We can't just pray, "Father, forgive me," and move on. Adoration is about building God up; confession is about tearing you down. David's confession gives us a model for what God desires from us when we go to Him in prayer. He wants down-on-your-knees, honest heartbreak.

I'm the first to say this place of brokenness is difficult to enter. It requires soul-searching. You have to face yourself in the mirror, and then you have to own up to your sin. But the truth is that any confession less than one that forces you to look inside your heart doesn't clear the room. Too many of us don't take the time to ask God to examine our hearts and, like David, pray, "Cleanse me from all unrighteousness and renew a right spirit within me."

It's far too easy (yet worthless) to say, "I've sinned." Scripture gives us many examples of men and women who were quick to say, "I have sinned," yet their actions revealed insincerity in their hearts. Twice Pharaoh told Moses, "I have sinned" (Exod. 9:27; 10:16–17), but his unwillingness to release the Hebrews and commanding his armies to chase them and return them to Egypt tells us his confession wasn't genuine.

> Any confession less than one that forces you to look inside your heart doesn't clear the room.

Judas confessed his sin but didn't truly repent of it. And when the Pharisees and Sadducees went to John the Baptist for baptism, he saw that their confession was merely lip-service, and he just let them have it! He called them snakes—the epitome of deception and evil! I like how *The Message* tells the story:

> When John realized that a lot of Pharisees and Sadducees were showing up for a baptismal experience because it was becoming the popular thing to do, he exploded: "Brood of snakes! What do you think you're doing slithering down here to the river? Do you think a little water on your snakeskins is going to make any difference? It's your life that must change, not your skin! And don't think you can pull rank by claiming Abraham as father. Being a descendant of Abraham is neither here nor there. Descendants of Abraham are a dime a dozen. What counts is your life. Is it green and blossoming? Because if it's deadwood, it goes on the fire."
>
> —Matthew 3:7–10

Of course, we have lots of modern-day examples as well. We've all seen the teary-eyed confessions of singers, politicians, and televangelists only to realize sooner or later their words and their tears were only for show. None of these ancient or modern-day confessions ever led the confessors to a broken place. If our confession is sincere, it will bring us to our knees. God tells us to look inside our hearts and humbly come to Him, confessing our wrongs and asking forgiveness: "Forgive me, God, for my thoughts; forgive me for my actions. I know there's no good thing in my flesh. O God, I confess." Taking ownership of your sin removes the spirit of pride.

When I think of pride, I always remember Paul's warning in Romans 12:3: "For by the grace given me I say to every one of you: Do not think of yourself more highly than you ought, but rather think of yourself with sober judgment, in accordance with the faith God has distributed to each of you." Confession compels you to admit you're not as high as you thought you were. You can't go to God boasting or with a hardened spirit.

One of the things that messes me up every time I read it is the account of Israel's first king, Saul, and how his hardened spirit and pride led to his self-inflicted death. Saul committed suicide on his sword because he wouldn't pray. He wouldn't admit his sin. He never cleared the room. First Chronicles 10:13–14 tells us: "Saul died because he was unfaithful to the LORD; he did not keep the word of the LORD and even consulted a medium for guidance, *and did not inquire of the LORD*" (emphasis added). What if Saul had just prayed?

Remember earlier when we talked about Peter and how he denied Jesus three times, even though he insisted he wouldn't? When Jesus told Peter that he would deny Him three times before the rooster crowed, Peter was incredulous. "I would *never* deny you," he told Jesus. And when it happened, Jesus looked at Peter as if to say, "I told you." Afterward, Peter saw Jesus waiting for him on the shore. I think we could say that Peter was in a place of brokenness, probably more broken than he'd ever felt or ever dreamed he'd be. But to go forward and be the man and church leader Jesus needed him to be, Peter needed to be broken. In prayer, you need a broken moment.

I've had many broken moments in prayer, but I still remember my prayer in a particularly difficult time. Before I was a pastor, I was a youth leader, and every spring I led a conference in Chicago called the Inner-City Youth Spring Break Conference. For ten years straight, we ministered to teenagers from all over the city. It was a huge event—the last one we held drew ten thousand teenagers to Navy Pier, a popular attraction in Chicago. Every year, sponsors and advertisers contributed tens of thousands of dollars to pay for the event. But toward the end, I was struggling to raise the money.

At a point, I was literally begging people for funds. I was calling people I never thought I'd have to call. God had always come through for us in the past. But it just became more difficult. And I remember saying to God, "OK, You win. There's nothing left in me. If there was any pride, it's gone. If there is any sense of righteousness, it's gone. If I thought I was anything, it's gone. If I am the hindrance, then forgive me. If I have taken credit, glory, and applause from You, forgive me. I have been brought to the lowest point."

I was in a broken place. I needed to die to myself.

That's why Paul says in 1 Corinthians 15:13, "I die daily" (NKJV). Paul knew he had to stay in a broken place. Each and every day, our flesh has to be put to death. I read a book recently that talked about confession and how in the Old Testament before the high priest could go into the holy of holies, where God's presence dwelled, he had to put blood on his ears, his thumbs, and his toes. You can't make this stuff up. Check it out:

> Moses also brought Aaron's sons forward and put some of the blood on the lobes of their right ears, on the thumbs of their right hands and on the big toes of their right feet. Then he splashed blood against the sides of the altar.
>
> —LEVITICUS 8:24

To enter God's presence, the priest had to smell like death, like a sacrifice. God was basically saying, "I can't smell *you*. I need to smell death." Before God could hear the priest, he needed to be "dead," broken. God wants that aroma of brokenness in our prayers. It's pleasing to Him. When we don't confess, we become self-reliant and confident in ourselves, not our Master. I imagine there have been times in your life when you knew you didn't respond correctly. You didn't pass the test. You reveled in your pride. Like David, the guilt festered inside you. Remember that—it's the place of brokenness.

SOME THINGS TO REMEMBER IN CONFESSION

Sometimes as I prepare to clear the room, it helps me to think through what God has told us about confession in His Word. Use the following list to help you offer sincere confession as you humble yourself before the throne.

Take ownership.

In the first three verses of Psalm 51, David uses the word "my," taking ownership of his sin: "my transgressions," "my iniquity," "my sin." He didn't blame others, and we mustn't either. When you take ownership of something, you take responsibility for it.

Make no excuses.

God doesn't want to hear your excuses or listen to you try to rationalize your sin like Adam did—"Well, God, it was that woman You gave me who caused me to sin." (See Genesis 3:12.) God desires honest confession. He's seeking broken hearts willing to be transparent and used by Him.

Be specific.

In your honesty, force yourself to be specific about your sin. You need to acknowledge it before yourself and before God. Offer a true apology. Remember, it's not enough to say, "I've sinned." That's what Pharaoh and the Pharisees said. A sincere heart offers a sincere confession.

Claim God's grace.

Remember 1 John 1:9: "If we confess our sins, he is faithful and just and will forgive us our sins and purify us from all unrighteousness." Look what happens when we confess. We're forgiven and cleansed. The dots connect: confession → forgiveness → cleansed heart. It's a beautiful, redemptive picture God has painted, and it's His promise to us.

Move on to thankfulness.

Don't get stuck and wallow in your sin. Wallowing never got anyone anywhere. Notice that 1 John 1:9 doesn't say we need to "beg" or "plead" for forgiveness. We offer honest and sincere confession, and He forgives. When you confess your sins to God, you've cleared the room. God has taken away your iniquity—as far as the east is from the west. Now you're ready to move on with a pure heart to the *T* in ACTSI: thankfulness.

LET'S TALK

- What role has confession played in your prayer life?
- How do you think honest confession can strengthen your prayer life?
- When you think about "going to an uncomfortable place of brokenness," what's your initial response? (Be honest with yourself.)
- Have you ever "wallowed" in unconfessed sin? How did you get out of the muck and mire?
- Have you experienced the power of "clearing the room"? If so, how did it change your prayers and relationship with God? If not, how do you think it would impact your prayer life?

Chapter 6

THE POWER OF RECALL

How Does Thankfulness Deepen Our Faith?

Rejoice always, pray without ceasing, give thanks in all circumstances; for this is the will of God in Christ Jesus for you.
—1 THESSALONIANS 5:16–18, ESV

THEY HAD LIVED with the infectious disease all their lives. The dreaded sickness ran through their bodies, and they had become accustomed to seeing their skin crusted over with lesions, their faces disfigured, and their limbs twisted. They knew the pain of being banished from friends and neighbors. They were used to crying out, "Unclean." Yet it didn't hurt any less each time they had to warn others of their presence. But that day, they had heard that Jesus was in their midst—Jesus, the Miracle Worker, the One who healed.

Matthew 17 tells us that when this group of ten lepers saw Jesus on His way to Jerusalem, they stood at a distance and cried out, "Jesus, Master, have pity on us!" (v. 13). Their cries stopped Jesus in His tracks. Now, don't miss this: Before these lepers cried out for Jesus to have pity on them and heal them, they called Him "Jesus, Master." They acknowledged who He was.

The lepers braved the sneers and humiliation that came

with going into the public square, hoping that maybe this day they would receive a miracle and be healed from this debilitating disease, that they would finally find physical and emotional relief and new lives. But their first words for Jesus weren't, "Heal us." First, they honored Him by shouting His name and then His position. They adored Him. Jesus heard them, and Luke 17:14 tells us that as they went away, all of them were healed.

But the story isn't over (and I think this is why we even have this story recorded in Scripture). When he saw he was healed, one of the lepers turned back to find Jesus while the other nine went on their way. When this man saw Jesus, he threw himself at His feet and in a loud voice praised and thanked Him. I can imagine the scene. Everyone's watching him, slowly recognizing him as the "leper." He's crying out, still somewhat in shock, weeping tears of joy, falling at Jesus' feet. Finally, Jesus gets to speak and asks, "Were there not ten cleansed? Where are the other nine?" Then Jesus looks down at the man and tells him, "Arise, your faith has made you"—and this is key—"*whole*." (See Luke 17:17–19, KJV.) The nine other lepers went away only physically healed, but this man's faith healed him spiritually and made him *holy*, set apart. This man who gave thanks got what the other nine never received. And it came only through gratitude. Growing up, my grandmother would say, "Thank you makes room for more because as you thank Him, He begins to prepare you to receive even more." The healed man's expression and words of thankfulness made room for more.

Your Testimony in Prayer

As we move on from confession and a place of brokenness, we thank God for everything He has done in our lives. That's why we have to be taught how to pray because we need to be taught to thank Him. It's a discipline that's core to our communication with God. In thankfulness, we focus on what God has done in us, for us, and through us.

> Thank you makes room for more because as you thank Him, He begins to prepare you to receive even more.

When I think about the leper who was healed and went back to thank Jesus, I wonder what the rest of this man's life looked like. Whatever became of the man, I do know this: he had an amazing testimony! His story of being healed and running back to thank Jesus became his awesome testimony of faith. That's how we can think about thankfulness in prayer—as our testimony. Every time we practice gratitude, we testify of God's goodness and power.

Thankfulness is our track record of what Jesus has done in our lives. It's like pulling out a list before you go any further in prayer—kind of like the actors do when they win an Oscar and go up to make their acceptance speech. They pull out a list of people to thank for their involvement and blessing in their lives. In prayer, we take time to recall what God has done: "*You did this and You did this, and I'm grateful You did this.*" Just like with adoration, one word of gratitude fuels the other.

I like to say that thankfulness makes us blessings-aware. When you spend time praising God for what He has done, is doing, and will do, you let God know you're aware of the blessings He has rained, and is raining, down on you. You're telling God you know and fully believe, as we read in James 1:17, that "every good and perfect gift is from above, coming down from the Father of the heavenly lights, who does not change like shifting shadows."

I'll add that it's also the polite thing to do. It shows that we value God. He desires our thankfulness. He responds to our gratitude. If you have kids, you probably remember teaching them to say thank you pretty much as soon as they could talk. You worked hard to instill manners. Imagine if you kept doing something for me and I never said thank you. That would be so rude and disrespectful. I've seen parents with two kids, one who has a spirit of entitlement and the other who is appreciative of everything that's done for them. The contrast is stark.

The executive pastor at our church, Pastor Jerome Glenn, has a son named Johnny who is always beyond thankful. If you give Johnny anything, he's just beside-himself happy, almost turning somersaults: "Oh my God, thank you so much!" He's been asking for a phone for a long time, and he finally got one. You should've heard him. "A phone! A phone!" And he just broke down in tears. I've told his dad, "Do not bring this kid near me, because I will give him everything." That because he's just so thankful for his blessings. God feels the same way when we show our overflowing gratitude to Him.

I know it may be easy to gloss over this discipline and think, "I've got this." You may even want to skip to supplication and intercession. But this part of prayer is essential. Why else do you think God's Word talks about thankfulness in more than one hundred verses?[1] He puts high priority on this discipline because He knows it changes us and our communication with Him—especially in our trials.

God Is God

Seven times hotter than normal. Flames so fiery they killed the soldiers as they threw the three Hebrew men into the furnace. When we think of Shadrach, Meshach, and Abednego, we remember the miracle God performed, the angel He sent—the "fourth man" in the furnace with them—and that all three friends walked out completely unsinged. They didn't even smell of smoke.

But let's back up a little before the miracle and look at what happened right before the command to heat up the furnace seven times hotter. The ruler of the Babylonians, King Nebuchadnezzar, had erected a ninety-foot golden statue and ordered all of the leaders in the province to bow down to it and worship it. The consequences for not following orders were clear: "Anyone who does not kneel and worship shall be thrown immediately into a roaring furnace" (Dan. 3:6, MSG).

It wasn't long before it was obvious that the three Hebrew men—who were placed in leadership positions after Babylon conquered Jerusalem and captured God's people—weren't following orders. Shadrach, Meshach, and Abednego said no. Actually, they said way more than no. In the biggest trial of their life, they basically said that no matter what happens, they'll go on record saying God is God. I'd say these three men had unshakable faith. Look at their words to Nebuchadnezzar.

> Shadrach, Meshach, and Abednego answered King Nebuchadnezzar, "Your threat means nothing to

> us. If you throw us in the fire, the God we serve can rescue us from your roaring furnace and anything else you might cook up, O king. But even if he doesn't, it wouldn't make a bit of difference, O king. We still wouldn't serve your gods or worship the gold statue you set up."
>
> —DANIEL 3:16–18, MSG

Thankfulness in the midst of a trial tells God that no matter what, you know He's on the throne and that you won't allow what you're going through to shake you and make you question if He's God. One of the things that always scares me is when people have a petition before the Lord and say, "Now, if He does this, then I know He's God." That's dangerous. You're basically saying that His response to your request defines Him as God. The enemy would like nothing better than to see you put God on probation. But He was God yesterday, and He's God today and forever. He's the One who was and is and is to come. Our responsibility—our privilege—is to acknowledge He is God and thank Him for what He's done, what He's doing, and what He will do in your life.

I'm not saying sincere thankfulness is easy. Just like with honest confession that takes us to a broken place, few of us want to be thankful in our trials. Even fewer want to thank God *for* the refining fire we may be walking in. Scripture doesn't tell us to be thankful *for* everything. I'm not thankful for my mother's sickness and death—far from it. But Paul does tell us to be thankful *in* everything. In his letter to the persecuted church in Thessalonica, Paul says, "Rejoice always, pray without ceasing, give thanks in *all* circumstances; for this is the will of God in Christ

Jesus for you" (1 Thess. 5:16–18, ESV, emphasis added). James even exhorts us to "count it all joy" when we have trials (Jas. 1:2, ESV).

How do we get to that place of thankfulness beyond our circumstances? When I'm walking through a trial, I recall what God has done in my life to bring me through other fires I've encountered. Saying thank you in the midst of the pain and remembering what God has done in your life keep you focused on Jesus, not the trial you're walking through. It's not just smart; it's also biblical! In Psalm 73, the psalmist talks about a treacherous point he faced in life. He says in essence, "As for me, my feet almost slipped, based on what I was going through. When I saw the prosperity of the wicked, I was envious. They have no struggles. Their bodies are healthy and strong. They are free from common burdens. And they are not plagued by human illness." (See Psalm 73:2–5.)

The psalmist was looking at the wicked and how they seemed to have it made while he was over there going through hell on earth. And then in verses 17 and 18 he says that when he entered the sanctuary of God, he understood the wicked's final destiny: that they are cast down to ruin. Then the psalmist looks back and realizes how good God has been to him, and he becomes thankful in the midst of his trial. I love this passage:

> Yet I am always with you; you hold me by my right hand. You guide me with your counsel, and afterward you will take me into glory. Whom have I in heaven but you? And earth has nothing I desire besides you. My flesh and my heart may fail, but God is the strength of my heart and my portion forever....

> It is good to be near God. I have made the Sovereign LORD my refuge; I will tell of all your deeds.
>
> —PSALM 73:23–26, 28

This "looking back" exercise is so important for growing in thankfulness, and it becomes such a foothold for us when we have trouble. And we *will* have trouble. Let's look at a verse in Lamentations 3. The writer starts out in deep despair, saying he has "seen trouble…coming from the lash of God's anger" (v. 1, MSG). And then he just makes a running list. For eighteen verses, he goes on and on about how excruciatingly horrible life has been. He even says that God "ground my face into the gravel…[and] pounded me into the mud" (v. 16, MSG). This guy has had a year (or more)!

And then we get to verse 20. He says he'll never forget the trouble and that he remembers the feeling of hitting rock bottom. And then he says, "But there's one *other* thing I remember." (v. 21, MSG, emphasis added). The King James Version says, "This I recall to my mind, therefore have I hope." This is what I'm talking about, the recall that has to happen in our minds and hearts to be able to walk in gratitude and then hope. The psalmist goes on to say:

> GOD's loyal love couldn't have run out, his merciful love couldn't have dried up. They're created new every morning. How great your faithfulness! I'm sticking with GOD (I say it over and over). He's all I've got left.
>
> —LAMENTATIONS 3:22–24, MSG

Recalling the times God brought you through a trial gives you hope to get to supplication. This writer is broken, crying out, ready to give up. But the recall takes him to a place of thankfulness: "It's because of the Lord's mercy that I am not consumed, that I'm not dead," he reminds himself. "Great is Thy faithfulness." Thankfulness positions him to see that God is faithful.

So what does all of this look like for us? Like the psalmist, you must remember *not to focus on what you're going through but to recall everything God has done.* When you look back on your life, what has God brought you through? If He has walked with you through so much already, you know He'll walk, or even carry, you through the pain you have today. We can draw a straight line from thankfulness to faithfulness to hope. It's about hindsight.

Don't skip over thankfulness in your communication with God. It's part of talking to Him. Following are some of my favorite scriptures about God's goodness. I encourage you to use them to help you express your gratitude to God. (I've also listed them in Appendix B for easy reference.)

> With praise and thanksgiving they sang to the LORD: "He is good; his love toward Israel endures forever." And all the people gave a great shout of praise to the LORD, because the foundation of the house of the LORD was laid.
>
> —EZRA 3:11

> I will give thanks to the LORD because of his righteousness; I will sing the praises of the name of the LORD Most High.
>
> —PSALM 7:17

I will give thanks to you, Lord, with all my heart; I will tell of all your wonderful deeds.

—Psalm 9:1

I will give you thanks in the great assembly; among the throngs I will praise you.

—Psalm 35:18

I will praise God's name in song and glorify him with thanksgiving.

—Psalm 69:30

Come, let us sing for joy to the Lord; let us shout aloud to the Rock of our salvation. Let us come before him with thanksgiving and extol him with music and song. For the Lord is the great God, the great King above all gods.

—Psalm 95:1–3

Enter his gates with thanksgiving and his courts with praise; give thanks to him and praise his name. For the Lord is good and his love endures forever; his faithfulness continues through all generations.

—Psalm 100:4–5

Praise the Lord. Give thanks to the Lord, for he is good; his love endures forever.

—Psalm 106:1

Let them give thanks to the Lord for his unfailing love and his wonderful deeds for mankind. Let them sacrifice thank offerings and tell of his works with songs of joy.

—Psalm 107:21–22

Give thanks to the LORD, for he is good; his love endures forever.

—PSALM 118:1

I thank and praise you, God of my ancestors: You have given me wisdom and power, you have made known to me what we asked of you, you have made known to us the dream of the king.

—DANIEL 2:23

Be filled with the Spirit, speaking to one another with psalms, hymns, and songs from the Spirit. Sing and make music from your heart to the Lord, always giving thanks to God the Father for everything, in the name of our Lord Jesus Christ.

—EPHESIANS 5:18–20

Do not be anxious about anything, but in every situation, by prayer and petition, with thanksgiving, present your requests to God. And the peace of God, which transcends all understanding, will guard your hearts and your minds in Christ Jesus.

—PHILIPPIANS 4:6–7

So then, just as you received Christ Jesus as Lord, continue to live your lives in him, rooted and built up in him, strengthened in the faith as you were taught, and overflowing with thankfulness.

—COLOSSIANS 2:6–7

Let the peace of Christ rule in your hearts, since as members of one body you were called to peace. And be thankful. Let the message of Christ dwell among you richly as you teach and admonish one another with all wisdom through psalms, hymns, and songs from the Spirit, singing to God with gratitude in your hearts. And whatever you do, whether in word or deed, do it all in the name of the Lord Jesus, giving thanks to God the Father through him.

—Colossians 3:15–17

Devote yourselves to prayer, being watchful and thankful.

—Colossians 4:2

Rejoice always, pray continually, give thanks in all circumstances; for this is God's will for you in Christ Jesus.

—1 Thessalonians 5:16–18

Therefore, since we are receiving a kingdom that cannot be shaken, let us be thankful, and so worship God acceptably with reverence and awe, for our "God is a consuming fire."

—Hebrews 12:28–29

Through Jesus, therefore, let us continually offer to God a sacrifice of praise—the fruit of lips that openly profess his name. And do not forget to do good and to share with others, for with such sacrifices God is pleased.

—Hebrews 13:15–16

Consider it pure joy, my brothers and sisters, whenever you face trials of many kinds, because you know that the testing of your faith produces perseverance. Let perseverance finish its work so that you may be mature and complete, not lacking anything.

—James 1:2–5

By now, I hope you understand that prayer is much more than asking for your needs to be met. I'm praying that's crystal clear for you now. But part of our communication with the omniscient and omnipotent God we worship and serve *is* praying for our needs and others'. God tells us to come to Him in prayer with our cares and our concerns. First John 5:14 says, "Now this is the confidence that we have in Him, that if we ask anything according to His will, He hears us" (NKJV). You've worshipped God in adoration, you've cleared the room in confession, and you've recalled His goodness in thankfulness. You have His attention; He has settled in. Now it's time to move on to the "asking" in supplication and intercession.

Let's Talk

- Why do you think thankfulness is such an important part of prayer?
- Have you ever had an experience when you trusted God even when He didn't respond the way you wanted Him to? What happened? If it led to a powerful testimony, share that story with someone today.
- How has gratitude, especially in the face of trials, changed your perspective?
- Look at the list of thankfulness-related verses in this chapter or Appendix B. What are some of your favorites? What do your favorite verses in this list mean to you? How can you use them in your prayer life to deepen your faith and trust?

Chapter 7

WRAPPED IN PRAYER

How Do We Present Our Supplication to God?

Delight yourself in the LORD, and He will give you the desires and petitions of your heart.
—PSALM 37:4, AMP

HE WAS USED to being in control. A well-known synagogue official, Jairus organized the schedule of services in the two-story, ornate building that was the most significant landmark in Capernaum, one of the largest and wealthiest cities in Israel. But now all his power and popularity meant nothing. His twelve-year-old daughter was sick, and he was just a helpless father whose wealth and influence couldn't change the fact that his only daughter was dying.

But Jairus had one possible lifeline. Jesus was back in Galilee and would be traveling through his city. If he could just get to Him… Mark's Gospel tells us that Jairus worked his way through the large crowd, and once he reached Jesus, he fell at His feet. In desperation, he told Jesus his need and asked (begged, for all practical purposes) Him to go to his home and lay hands on his daughter, fully believing Jesus could and would heal her.

> Then one of the synagogue leaders, named Jairus, came, and when he saw Jesus, he fell at his feet. He pleaded earnestly with him, "My little daughter is dying. Please come and put your hands on her so that she will be healed and live." So Jesus went with him.
>
> —MARK 5:22–24

If you remember the story, a few things happened before Jesus reached Jairus' daughter. On the way to the ruler's house, Jesus stopped to heal a woman who had been hemorrhaging for twelve years. As He was speaking to the woman, messengers arrived to tell Jairus his daughter was dead. But Jesus didn't skip a beat. He immediately reached out to the heartbroken father, telling him, "Don't be afraid; just believe" (v. 36). Jesus assured Jairus that his daughter would be fine. And in verse 41, Jesus raised her from the dead, knocking the mourners and scoffers off their feet and to their knees.

It's one of those stories in Scripture that reminds me to go to Jesus in prayer, humble myself, and ask for what I need. When everything is breaking loose, we can run to Jesus like Jairus did and in prayer tell Him what's happening. In the ACTSI tool we've been working through, this is called supplication. But let me be clear. There's a reason the verb *supplicate* comes from a Latin term, *supplicare*, that means "to kneel."[1] Supplication isn't groveling or rubbing the genie's magic lamp. In supplication, we ask from a place of humility. I think about the children of Israel and how they worshipped idols until finally, in humble desperation, they begged the Lord to forgive them: "Then the Israelites cried out to the LORD, 'We have sinned against you, forsaking our God and serving the Baals'" (Judg. 10:10). When they humbled themselves and repented, God heard them.

Are you starting to see how all the dots connect? When you begin your prayer with adoration, confession, and thankfulness, you're already in a humble place by the time you come to supplication to make your needs known. You're already at His feet. You've adored Him, cleared the room, and thanked Him for His blessings, and now you're ready to present your petition to God with confidence. Once we've come to this place, He tells us, "*Now* tell Me, what do you want? Give Me your list of things you want from Me. You have not because you ask not."

How You Go to God Matters

When Jairus went to Jesus, he was specific and clear. He said, "Please come and put your hands on her so that she will be healed and live" (Mark 5:23). Nehemiah also made a specific request when he stood in front of King Artaxerxes. The king saw his cupbearer's grief over the destruction of Jerusalem and asked Nehemiah, "So tell me, what can I do for you?" Nehemiah prayed and then clearly presented his petition to the king: "Let me go back to Judah so that I can rebuild the city of my ancestors." (See Nehemiah 2:5.) Then Nehemiah even asked for letters to certain governors requesting protection and wood for the rebuilding effort. (See Nehemiah 2:7–9.)

God asks us to be clear and specific in our requests: In Mark 5, Jairus said, "Come to my house and heal my daughter." The two blind men in Matthew 20 said, "Give us sight." In John 11, Mary and Martha asked Jesus, "Raise our brother." In 2 Kings 20, Hezekiah prayed, "Give me more time." And as we just saw in Judges 10, the people of Israel cried out, "Forgive us!"

When everything is breaking loose, we can run to Jesus and in prayer tell Him what we need.

Our Lord also asks us to come to Him and present our petition with confidence. So many times, we make our requests without real confidence. We present our needs shrouded in doubt and fear. I can only imagine what it was like for Jairus as he pressed through the crowds in anguish to get to Jesus; he believed Jesus could heal his daughter. In fact, did you catch what happened when Jairus received the news from his messenger? Assured by Jesus, Jairus pressed on confidently in the midst of the pain. It's a lot like the blind men in Matthew 20 doing whatever they needed to do to get Jesus' attention, believing that if they could just get Him to look their way, they would be healed. They acted in faith. God tells us, "I need you to come to Me with your requests correctly," because when you come to Jesus correctly—approaching the throne confidently, believing He is who He says He is and that He's able to provide—trust me, it's a whole other thing.

When we humbly and clearly bring our cares to God with confidence, He often uses our time with Him to heal our souls and refuel us—and He does all this through prayer. I'll be painfully transparent with you. So many times, my supplication comes in cries of pain. Being in this seat of leadership in the church has caused some of the deepest hurts and disappointments I've experienced in my life. What's worse is that I can't say or do anything in response to the attacks and injustices I've had to endure. Like Job, I just have to take one blow after the other. Honestly, I can understand why some church leaders have turned to alcohol or drug use. I can understand why some have walked away, abandoning their assignments.

God often uses our time with Him to heal our souls and refuel us.

I remember one specific time in ministry that was so hurtful I just wanted to quit. I was at a ministry retreat meeting one of my brothers in Christ, Choco De Jesús, for coffee, and I was just honest. "I don't want to do this anymore," I told him. "I don't want to build relationships. I don't want to pour into others or do any more mentoring." The ridicule and criticism hurled against me had brought me to a boiling point. When you're a pastor, you quickly learn that sheep have teeth—and those teeth are sharp! At times, you can feel as if you've been good to the sheep—you've fed the sheep and given your life to them. But you're quickly turned on and bitten. My friend understood and reminded me, "As leaders of His flock, that's what we live to do. We live to pour. Anytime we're not pouring ourselves out, we're not living."

I knew he was right. But how do you take a pitcher that you turned upside down, saying, "I'm done; no more," and turn it back up to be filled once again? At the retreat that night as we worshipped and prayed, I told God, "OK, fill me back up, and I'll pour again." When we enter into His gates with thanksgiving and His courts with praise, we find the strength, the help we need to continue to do what needs to be done. It all happens in prayer.

The best example of this is when Jesus was praying in

the Garden of Gethsemane and said, "Lord, take this cup from Me." The Bible says Jesus was in so much anguish He sweat drops of blood. Three times Jesus asked His Father to spare Him the cross. But because He stayed in prayer, Jesus was able to get up from His knees and say, "OK, let's go." He left the garden with a peace that passes all human understanding and a strength that wasn't His own. We're not going to get any of this without prayer. We can go to God feeling one way and leave feeling like, "I can do this." The Holy Spirit uses our time with Him to work in our minds and hearts. I love God's words to Paul when he was pleading with Him to take away the "thorn in his flesh": "And He said to me, 'My grace is sufficient for you, for My strength is made perfect in weakness'" (1 Cor. 12:9, KJV). Our Savior's supernatural strength is not perfected in us until we are completely weak.

At times I can get so lost in adoration, confession, and thankfulness that by the time I get to supplication, I might not even present my petition. Sometimes Jesus' words to the disciples come to mind, "Your Father knows what you need before you ask him" (Matt. 6:8). And I just say, "Lord, You know." Other times, I realize that what I thought I needed Him to do in someone else is really about Him changing my heart.

And still there are other times when even after I've adored Him, confessed my sin, and thanked Him, I'm still so broken by the blows and disappointment of ministry with no real revelation. I've felt a lot like Elijah after he heard that Queen Jezebel vowed to kill him. (See 1 Kings 19.) He was so frustrated and scared that he just went into the wilderness, lay down under a tree, and asked God to take him. "I've had enough, Lord," he said. Elijah was in a broken place. The blows and disappointments of ministry had decimated him. He was exhausted. I know that feeling. You may know it too. Soon God provided food and protection so Elijah could rest, and He did this not once but twice. God gave Elijah what He knew His prophet needed to continue the journey.

I can honestly say the *only* thing that has allowed me to survive has been my prayer life and my village of people who pray with me. If I didn't have those, I wouldn't be here. Without prayer, I'd be done (like Elijah was). Prayer brings me into God's presence. And when I enter in, I know I can come broken, humbly present my petition to my Savior, and come out with what I need to continue.

Treasures of the Heart

Through supplication, God gives us the opportunity to develop a deep connection with Him, because there's nothing like a secret to create intimacy in a relationship. When only one other person knows something about you, it can't help but make the relationship feel special. I'm talking about the secret petitions you present in your prayers, the deep desires that are between you and God. Psalm 37 tells us, "Delight yourself in the Lord, and He will give you the desires and *petitions* of your heart" (v. 4, AMP, emphasis added). These are the petitions you hide away and give God exclusive access to—the treasures of your heart.

I think of Mary when the shepherds told her about the angels they had seen and the world-changing message they had heard. The shepherds were amazed by the magnificent scene they had witnessed, and they told everyone about it. But Mary was calm when she heard their account. Luke's Gospel says she "treasured up all these things and pondered them in her heart" (Luke 2:19). She kept it all to herself, and I'm sure in the days, weeks, and years that followed, Mary reflected often on that night and the petitions she hid in her heart.

When we keep God's words in our hearts, treasuring and pondering them, we remind ourselves to believe. It's like the recall we talked about in chapter 6. In our supplication, we recall our words to Him about our secret petitions and His words to us. I like that the Greek word for "treasured" is *suntéreó*; it also means "keep safe."[2] In hindsight, I can see how God has kept my secret petitions safe and at the right time began to answer my prayer openly before others. People would see and think, "Wow, look what God did," but they didn't know how long I'd been carrying my petition.

Early in my life, I knew I had been called to be a pastor. I hadn't talked about it because some people could see me only as a youth leader. Some people could see me only as an "armor-bearer" (the pastor's right arm or attendant). So being called to pastor and lead a church was something I kept between God and me. I just held it. I treasured it in my heart and wrapped it in prayer.

In Scripture, we see many examples of leaders who were called at an early age but hid the desire in their heart. I think about Elisha and wonder about the secret petitions of his heart. When God released Elijah from his service as a prophet, God told Elijah that He had appointed Elisha to serve as the new voice to His people. But what we don't know is what Elisha had been carrying in his heart all his life. Growing up, tending his father's fields, was there a part of Elisha that had been praying secretly, "God, I know that You have more for me than this. God, help me to be patient with this field I'm working in. Give me the endurance to wait on You and not make a move by myself"?

When Elijah walked up to Elisha and threw his cloak over him, indicating his appointment as Elijah's successor and adoption as his son, Elisha dropped everything and followed his teacher. Could it be that Elijah had just shaken the secret petitions that had been living in Elisha's heart? Finally, here was the call that awakened years of hidden prayers. *This* was the day God publicly answered the secret petition of Elisha's heart. He had finished his old way of life and would now learn the ways of a prophet. Everything he had been praying for was coming to fruition.

Think about a time you kept a prayer just between you and God. Now think about a time when you didn't keep it hidden. What happened? Remember when Joseph shared what God had intended for his heart only? I believe part of Joseph's problems came from him sharing his petitions with his half brothers, who were already jealous of him. Imagine the scene. They're all sitting around the breakfast table one morning and out of the blue Joseph says, "Hey guys, let me tell you about my dream that has all of you bowing down to me one day." Talk about poor judgment and disobedience! His brothers left the table that day filled with hatred for him. But Joseph didn't learn his lesson. He couldn't wait to get to breakfast the next morning to tell his brothers about a second dream he had. This time the brothers, plus their father and mother, were doing the bowing. His half brothers hated him even more. My guess is at that point some of them started scheming to do away with this dreamer-brother of theirs for good.

Some things have to remain in your heart between you and God because the moment you speak them, you intensify the warfare. From the day Joseph stupidly shared the first dream, his life became a struggle. He was thrown into a well, sold as a slave, falsely accused of attempted rape, and sentenced to prison. Don't forget that the enemy is the prince of the power of the air (Eph. 2:2). He hears the requests you speak to others.

It took me years to learn that you can't say or share everything. I began to notice that at almost the moment I shared my secret petition with others, my warfare increased. The very moment I opened my mouth and spoke it, life became a little bit (sometimes a lot) harder. So I began to wrap these secret petitions in prayer.

WRAPPED IN PRAYER

Earlier, I mentioned my secret petition over my calling as a pastor. Thankfully, I wrapped that in prayer and said nothing. I kept it to myself. I kept praying, "OK. I know what You called me to do. I do not know how. I do not see it." But I just kept praying. I remember telling my wife I wanted to move to Alabama to lead a church because I didn't want to lead one in Chicago. My former pastor was in Chicago, and the church was there. I didn't want to lead with so much "familiar" around me. One day, a woman who knew me in my old church called and said, "If you are ready to start your church, I will pay for the rent on a building. I know that God has called you to do something. If you will do it, I will fund it."

What church planter gets that kind of opportunity? But remember, I had been wrapping my calling in prayer; it was between God and myself. So I took this opportunity to God, and in prayer the Lord told me, "No. If you start now, you can only repeat what you have seen, and there is more that I need to show you."

> Some things have to remain in your heart between you and God because the moment you speak them, you intensify the warfare.

So I stayed in Chicago. I was thirty-six when I sensed the Lord telling me, "*Now*, it's time to lead." That's when He sent me to Choco De Jesús, former senior pastor of New Life Covenant Church on the north side of Chicago. My wife and I joined Choco's church, and eventually I began to minister there. Choco confirmed the secret petition I'd been carrying for so long. He said, "I see the calling in you. It does not scare me. It does not intimidate me. I want to *plant* it."

Those were his words. He saw what I had been carrying. It was my Elijah-Elisha moment! My heart leapt that day. The Bible says that when Elizabeth heard Mary's voice, the baby inside her womb, John the Baptist, leapt (Luke 1:41). When Elijah threw his cloak over Elisha, Elisha immediately jumped up. The calling and desire within him—what he had carried in silence for years—literally leapt for joy.

You have to keep wrapping your secret petitions—those hidden desires, callings, and requests—in prayer. Keep holding them and be sure to reveal them only to those who can help you deliver them, not to those who want to abort them. I didn't tell Pastor Choco, "I've been called to be a pastor." God prepared the way and revealed it to him. In hindsight, now I can see that if I had started the church that woman was willing to fund, the church would have been a preemie. It would have been a premature baby, and my struggles would have been greater.

This is key: *Every opportunity that comes to you is not a God opportunity.* A lot of us struggle with knowing what is or isn't a God opportunity. We all want to discern between the two. That's why you have to wrap your secret petition in prayer. Before I began to pastor, I was working as a juvenile probation officer, and the flexible schedule allowed me to pursue ministry. I basically could do what I wanted to do. I could move according to how I wanted to move. And then an opportunity came for me to work in the executive offices of Cook County. It was amazing. I would have a car and an office downtown with a view of the Chicago River. I would be driving from county to county. And I would be the only Black person in this seat.

Whoa! Seems like a slam dunk, right? Lights out! But remember, I had spent the last decade wrapping my calling in prayer. I'd spent years protecting and treasuring my secret petition. That night, I took the new job opportunity to God and He told me, "This is not your job. If you take this job, you will not be free to do what I have called you to do." The benefits didn't add up to freedom in the spirit. You have to be careful you don't allow money and possessions to be the only, or even a driving, factor in your decisions. If that's the case, all it takes is another offer. And let me tell you straight up, if money and benefits are all it takes to move you, then you are done, my friend.

I was with Pastor Choco, and we were working together. I knew I wasn't ready to be planted as the leader of a church yet. One weekend, I went to Atlanta to preach at a huge church's youth conference. The move of God was so powerful. Thousands of youth were filled with the

Holy Spirit. When I finished preaching, kids were slain in the Spirit all across the altar. The power of God was so heavy they had to carry kids to the buses. I was in a room changing clothes when someone knocked on the door and said, "The bishop would like to speak with you."

"I want to offer you a job to come down here and be my youth pastor," he said.

I quickly replied: "No, thank you."

"You are only saying no because I haven't told you how much I pay."

And I said to him, "I am saying no because I am confident this is not my destiny. I could come here and take your money, and I would only be here for a little while. I don't need to waste my time or yours because I know the direction of my destiny."

Why would I compromise the secret petition I had spent decades praying about? You can only sense what is or isn't a God opportunity when you know that in supplication, you've wrapped it in prayer.

We all want to know what is and isn't a secret petition, what we need to keep silent about and what we need to invite others to pray with us for. I tell people to keep secret the things that God puts in your spirit, in your heart, that are bigger than you. Look at what Joseph was dreaming about. His dreams said he was going to be the head of something so big that his family would bow down before him. When he had that dream, he was working in a field. How do you go from a field to a royal seat? His brothers couldn't fathom it. Even when he shared his second dream with his parents, his father, Jacob, was incredulous: "So you're saying that your mother and I are going to bow before you also?" (See Genesis 37:10.) Those things that are beyond you, beyond your resume, beyond your experience, beyond your village, and beyond your circle—keep those things secret, hidden away, and treasure them privately in your heart until God begins to publicly reveal them.

He Hears Your Ask

I want to leave this chapter assuring (or reminding) you that Jesus hears your petition. Just like He heard Jairus, the blind men, and the lepers. Just like the Lord heard Adam, Noah, Abraham, Moses, Joshua, Esther, Elijah, and Elisha. Just like the king heard Nehemiah. The list goes on.

> You can only discern what is or isn't a God opportunity when you know you've wrapped your petition in prayer.

When Jairus brought his request to Jesus, He didn't hesitate. Jesus went immediately with the hurting father to address his need. Even though the large crowd was pressing in, Jesus still took time to listen to Jairus and moved on his behalf. You can be confident that your Creator and Savior hears your prayers. That promise is repeated again and again in His Word.

> And when he prayed to him, the Lord was moved by his entreaty and listened to his plea.
>
> —2 Chronicles 33:13

> Then you will call on me and come and pray to me, and I will listen to you. You will seek me and find me when you seek me with all your heart.
>
> —Jeremiah 29:12–13

> Call to me and I will answer you and tell you great and unsearchable things you do not know.
>
> —Jeremiah 33:3

> Ask and it will be given to you; seek and you will find; knock and the door will be opened to you.
>
> —Matthew 7:7

> We know that God does not listen to sinners. He listens to the godly person who does his will.
>
> —John 9:31

> For the eyes of the Lord are on the righteous and his ears are attentive to their prayer.
>
> —1 Peter 3:12

> And if we know that he hears us—whatever we ask—we know that we have what we asked of him.
>
> —1 John 5:15

We've covered almost all of the ACTSI disciplines. I hope by now you're seeing how important it is to be taught to pray and how these disciplines work together to deepen our relationship with Jesus. In the next chapter, we'll be talking about intercession. I think you'll soon realize that interceding for others may look very different from what you thought. After you consider the questions below, turn the page with me.

Let's Talk

- What does it mean to you to go to God humbly but with confidence?

- What are some of the roadblocks that keep you from approaching God in confidence, believing He can and will answer your petition?
- What are some of the secret petitions you've held in your heart? Think back to when God began to answer them and thank Him for His goodness.
- How has wrapping some of your petitions in prayer helped you make decisions when opportunities or obstacles came along?
- Do you truly believe God listens to your asks? Why or why not? (Be honest.) List some verses that promise us God listens, and moves in response to our prayers. What can you do to cling to and grasp those truths?

Chapter 8

GETTING OTHERS IN FRONT OF JESUS

How Do We Intercede for Others With God's Will—not Ours—in Mind?

This is the confidence we have in approaching God: that if we ask anything according to his will, he hears us.
—1 John 5:14

Crash! Pieces of debris from the roof fell to the ground. As the crowd looked toward the ceiling, the four men continued with their mission, determined to get their friend in front of Jesus. I don't know how long these four friends dug before debris rained down on those who had gathered to see and listen to Jesus. But I do know that they dug long and hard enough to make a man-sized hole in the roof. I also know they had thought about it enough to ensure that when they lowered down their friend, Jesus would see him. The Bible tells us the mat came down "right in front of Jesus" (Luke 5:19, MSG).

All of the determination, all of the quick planning, all of the physical labor paid off. When Jesus saw the "bold faith" of these four friends, He looked at their paralyzed friend and said to him, "Get up. Take up your mat and walk." (See Luke 5:24.)

Of course, these four friends would have preferred to enter through the door. It would've been much easier. But when they saw the large crowds and realized it wasn't going to be a simple mission, they were innovative and audacious in their faith. "Our friend *will* be healed today," they determined. And "when Jesus saw their [active] faith [springing from confidence in Him], He said, 'Man, your sins are forgiven'" (Luke 5:20, AMP).

When I think about the fifth and final discipline in our ACTSI tool, this story recorded in Luke 5 and Mark 2 often comes to mind. I can just see these guys marching up to that house and realizing that they weren't going to be able to push through the throng of people that had gathered. I wonder how long it was before they got up enough gumption to climb up on the roof. I can see them silently making their way onto the roof, one after the other, together carrying the mat that held their paralyzed friend, the whole time praying that this would work, that no one would stop them. Then they squatted or got down on their knees to dig a hole large enough to float a person lying horizontally through. They didn't give up until they got their friend in front of Jesus. It's the perfect picture of intercession, the *I* in ACTSI, and of the desperation we often feel when we bring others to our Savior.

A Heart Check

I always say that intercession is a heart check, because it's not about you. It's almost like saying to God, "Now that I have Your attention, I'm not just here for me (supplication). I'm also here for [insert name]." When we intercede for someone else, we position ourselves between God and the object of our prayers. That's what the word *intercede* means: to go or pass between. That's what the paralyzed man's friends in Luke 5 did; they took it upon themselves to facilitate the encounter between him and Jesus.

> They didn't give up until they got their friend in front of Jesus. It's the perfect picture of intercession.

Remember the story about Moses interceding for Israel in Exodus 32? While Moses was on the mountain receiving the Ten Commandments, the people made a golden calf to worship. The Lord was beyond irate—He was ready to bring the fire down and destroy the people He had carried across the Red Sea. That's when Moses stood between Israel and God and begged Him to spare the people: "But Moses sought the favor of the LORD his God. 'LORD,' he said, 'why should your anger burn against your people, whom you brought out of Egypt with great power and a mighty hand?'" (v. 12). And then Moses said in verse 13, "Remember your servants Abraham, Isaac and Israel, to whom you swore by your own self."

Sometimes, such as in this case, an intercessor is the cosigner when your credit isn't good. The Israelites had destroyed their credit with God. Moses became their backup, their only hope. Other times, you just need someone to touch and agree with you. You need a cosigner in the spirit. When the paralyzed man's friends brought him to Jesus, they interceded for him. Anytime you ask your Savior to do something, it's a form of prayer. Put simply, "God, do me a favor" is the key line in intercession. It's the heart check. You're asking Him to move in someone else's life. You cannot be an intercessor and be selfish.

THE MARKS OF AN INTERCESSOR

Throughout Scripture, we see God's people interceding for others. I've been in both places: the interceder and the one who's the object of intercession. What I've realized from those experiences is that all intercessors bear certain marks.

> In intercession, we position ourselves between God and the object of our prayers.

An intimate relationship with Jesus. I love what God says after Moses finishes pleading for the Israelites: "And the LORD said to Moses, 'I will do the very thing you have asked because I am pleased with you, and *I know you by name*'" (Exod. 33:17, emphasis added). You don't usually go to someone and ask them to do something for you if you don't have a solid relationship with them. To intercede, we need an intimate relationship with Christ. I always think of Mary and Martha running to Jesus in John 11, interceding for their brother, Lazarus. They knew Jesus well. He had been to their house many times. Jesus wept for these people He loved—the people He knew by name—and He raised their brother from the grave.

An ability to feel and bear the weight. Having an intimate relationship with Jesus strengthens you to feel and bear the weight of the burden you're bringing to Him. Let's go back to the four men who did everything they could to get their paralyzed friend into the very room Jesus was standing in. They literally bore the weight of their friend and his illness as they carried him to the house and then took drastic action to get him onto the roof and carefully lower him down—all the while expectant of what Jesus would do. Sometimes when I'm interceding for someone, I can feel the weight of that person. I can feel what they're going through; they're heavy in my spirit. That's what an intercessor feels.

Unrelenting persistence. What would have happened had those four friends given up when they saw the large crowd and knew they'd never get through the door? The whole story would have changed. They wouldn't have broken through the roof, Jesus wouldn't have seen their faith, and their friend wouldn't have been healed. Intercession relies on unrelenting persistence. It builds up your faith, stretches you, and toughens you up. In Matthew 15, a tough woman went to Jesus on her knees, interceding on behalf of her daughter, begging Him to free her child from a demon. Jesus said to the Canaanite mother, "It's not fit to take the children's bread and throw it to a dog." And she basically said, "Truth, Lord. I'll be a dog. Then give me the crumbs that fall from the table." (See Matthew 15:26–27.) The woman had faith that all she needed was crumbs. She didn't even ask Jesus to go to her house. She believed that whatever power or attention He had to spare was enough. Jesus said her faith was great, and her daughter was healed that very hour—all because she persisted in her petition.

Laser focus. The four friends in Luke 5 weren't distracted by the crowd or the obstacles they encountered that day. Not only did they come up with the idea of lowering their friend through the roof, but they also figured out how to get up there and then how to execute their plan. It required a lot of engineering and laser focus to pull off. And my guess is that people outside saw what was happening on the roof. I can't imagine four guys digging through a roof without the crowd outside sending up questions, yells, and even taunts and threats. Focus is an essential mark of an intercessor.

A breakthrough mindset. When we intercede for others, we need to talk to God, believing that He will move. We must be confident that He'll break through—just as those four friends believed as they dug through the roof that if they could just create a hole big enough to get their friend to Jesus, he would be healed. We too must go to God with confidence.

When you intercede, do you go to God believing He knows your name? Do you feel the weight of the burden someone is carrying and persist in prayer? Do you avoid distractions and pray, believing for a breakthrough? Bottom line: Do you do whatever it takes to bring the person you're interceding for to Jesus?

GOD'S WILL VERSUS YOUR WILL

I want to make sure you understand something that you may have missed, something that will likely turn what you think about intercession on its ear. Intercession is not about your desires. As an intercessor you're not praying *your* will for someone. You're not trying to push God into handling a situation the way you want to see it handled. Instead, you're finding, cooperating with, and praying into God's will for that person. I want to be clear: "praying *into* God's will" means you're leaning into His will and praying according to God's plans for someone's life. True intercession is the desire to see the object of our prayers come into close fellowship with Christ.

When you intercede for others, you need to pray, believing for a breakthrough.

I'll be the first to say that's not always a comfortable place to be. The truth is that intercessors are always in that uncomfortable middle seat, that dreaded one everyone avoids. On an airplane, most of us run for the aisle or window seat because no one wants to be stuck in the middle. We're conditioned to avoid it and all its inconveniences. But when you intercede for someone, that's where you are. You're between that person and God. You're praying for God's will, not your own. It's what 1 John 5:14 tells us: "This is the confidence that we have toward Him, that if we ask anything *according to His will*, He hears us" (ESV, emphasis added). That means you're praying into God's established will for this person's life. See? I told you intercession may be different from what you thought.

When God called Jeremiah to be His prophet, He told Jeremiah, "Before I formed you in the womb I knew you, before you were born I set you apart" (Jer. 1:5). And later, in Jeremiah 29:11, God said, "For I know the plans I have for you...plans to prosper you and not to harm you, plans to give you hope and a future." We've been predestined, marked by God. His will is for us to know Him, and as intercessors we're called, and even required, to pray into that will.

In John 17, Jesus was the perfect example of intercession as He prayed for His disciples (both the ones who knew Him then and those who would come to know Him in the future):

> I do not pray for these alone but also for those who will believe in Me through their word; that they all may be one, as You, Father, are in Me, and I in You; that they also may be one in us, that the world may believe that You sent Me.
>
> —John 17:20–21, NKJV

Jesus prayed that God's purposes would be accomplished in the lives of His disciples. Instead, we tend to pray into our own desires, especially when we're interceding for someone. If someone is sick, we ask God to heal them. If someone needs a job, we ask God to send them employment. We read Jesus' promise in John 14:14—"If you ask anything in My name, I will do it" (NKJV)—and think we'll get everything we ask for. But there's often a vast difference between your ask and His will. And—listen to me here because you need to get this—*the only way you can go from your ask to His will is in prayer*, because in prayer, you lose yourself.

> As an intercessor, you're not praying for *your* will or your desires for someone. You're praying for God's.

Don't forget who you're praying to. You're talking to God the Father, the author and finisher of our faith. You're talking to the One who created us, who knows and unconditionally loves the person you're bringing to Jesus. Remember that you don't have all the information—the big picture—and never will. We don't even understand everything we see clearly, much less the unseen. So we have to pray knowing that God knows more (and better) than we do. We need faith in His perfect will.

One of the things I find amazing—I teach this often—is

that the children of Israel asked for a king. We all know that was not God's *perfect* will for them. But He allowed them to have what they wanted. That's the *permissive* will of God—when God allows you to have what you ask for and then you have to deal with the results of it. Think about all the kings, battles, wars, and even exile the Jews went through because of their request for an earthly king. Being in God's perfect will is when you literally accept what He desires for you. God permitted Israel to have a king, but it wasn't His perfect will.

Earlier, I shared about my mom dying. She had cancer. In the months leading up to her passing, I prayed, "OK, God, I'm asking for You to heal her. Please heal my mom." But then as I began to look at the situation—and things weren't getting better—I began to pray, "OK, so let me begin to pray Your will, because if things are not turning around, is there something else, God, that You're choosing to do right now?" I had to choose God's will over my own.

Praying Into God's Plans

Understanding what true intercession is will drastically change how you pray because you're seeking for God's will to be accomplished in someone else's life. How do we learn to pray for others according to His will? When we tell someone, "I'll pray for you," we're usually saying, "I'm going to pray for your needs." But sometimes their needs will not bring God's perfect will to fruition. Jesus teaches us the best way of praying into His will, and it doesn't happen with one prayer. We see the progression in the Garden of Gethsemane just before Jesus' arrest.

Jesus was overwhelmed, thinking about what would

happen in the coming days. So He took Peter, James, and John with Him to the garden to intercede with Him. Let's read the passage:

> Then Jesus went with his disciples to a place called Gethsemane, and he said to them, "Sit here while I go over there and pray." He took Peter and the two sons of Zebedee along with him, and he began to be sorrowful and troubled. Then he said to them, "My soul is overwhelmed with sorrow to the point of death. Stay here and keep watch with me."
>
> Going a little farther, he fell with his face to the ground and prayed, "My Father, if it is possible, may this cup be taken from me. Yet not as I will, but as you will."
>
> Then he returned to his disciples and found them sleeping. "Couldn't you men keep watch with me for one hour?" he asked Peter. "Watch and pray so that you will not fall into temptation. The spirit is willing, but the flesh is weak."
>
> He went away a second time and prayed, "My Father, if it is not possible for this cup to be taken away unless I drink it, may your will be done."
>
> When he came back, he again found them sleeping, because their eyes were heavy. So he left them and went away once more and prayed the third time, saying the same thing.
>
> Then he returned to the disciples and said to them, "Are you still sleeping and resting? Look, the hour has come, and the Son of Man is delivered into the hands of sinners. Rise! Let us go! Here comes my betrayer!"
>
> —Matthew 26:36–46

Look at how the whole time in the garden, Jesus was tapping into His Father's will. The first time He went to the disciples, He was on edge and scolded them, "What? Could you not pray with me one hour?" The second time, He was a bit calmer and said nothing to them when He found them asleep once again. The third time, He came back saying, "The hour is now." He was in a calm place. But that transcendent peace didn't come without continual prayer.

Understanding what true intercession is will drastically change how you pray.

I love what that tells us about the peace that passes all understanding (Phil. 4:7). How many times have I prayed for that kind of peace? I'm sure you have too. In some of the stories I've read about Christians who were persecuted for their faith, the believers talk about experiencing peace while being physically attacked. I think God gives them supernatural peace. He knows they're suffering in His name. We get this kind of non-human peace through prayer. You have to keep going back to God until your spirit settles for whatever His will demands.

Don't miss this. Jesus' acceptance of His Father's will didn't come without incredible anguish. The Bible says He sweat drops of blood. That's what pressing into God's perfect will often looks like, because it takes a while for your ideas, your desires and passions, to die. That kind of surrender comes only through time spent with God. No flesh can glory in the light of His presence. The more we get into the presence of God, like John the Baptist said we decrease and He increases (John 3:30).

One of the stories in Scripture that always blows my

mind is Naomi and Ruth's. When Ruth's mother-in-law, Naomi, left Judah for Moab, she was full but she returned empty. She left with her husband, Elimelek, and two sons and returned to Judah with only her daughter-in-law Ruth. This woman had held three funerals. She'd buried her husband and two sons. When Naomi returned, the women came out to celebrate her, "Can this be Naomi?" And she quickly said, "Don't call me Naomi. Call me Mara [which means "bitter"], because the Almighty has made my life very bitter" (Ruth 1:20). Naomi had not tapped into the will of God yet. She didn't understand what God was up to. She couldn't see the big picture—until Ruth became pregnant and handed her the child who would be part of the lineage of Jesus.

But what did Naomi have to endure to get the blessing? She had to experience the bitterness and loss. She had to embrace it all so she could literally hold the will of God in her arms. It's OK to go through these difficult phases, but you can't stay there. You have to look for God. You have to look for His will in your life and others' lives—in the midst of your grief, in the midst of your loss, in the midst of your disappointment. It's a very difficult seat, because we're taught to want to be in control.

I'll admit this is when it gets really, really scary. In the Book of Job, we see Job's wife watching him get pummeled by one trial after another. He loses his life—all his children, all his servants, all his livestock. And then he finds his body covered with painful sores that he scrapes with a broken piece of pottery. I'm cringing as I think about it. The scene is horrific. And at one point, Job's wife tells him, "Just curse God and die." (See Job 2:9.) Essentially, she was saying, "I can't take seeing you like this. So why don't you just go ahead and give up?" She couldn't sit in the seat as Job's intercessor because she couldn't get past her own feelings of grief.

Realizing his wife couldn't truly intercede for him, Job responded to her question: "Shall we accept the good from God and not the bad?" (See Job 2:10.) Basically, he's telling her, "Back up! You can't intercede for me right now. Let me stay in the seat in the face of God and go before God by myself." Job's friends weren't able to intercede for him either. Remember? They sat with Job seven days and nights, saying absolutely nothing at first because they had no idea what to say. They were too busy trying to understand what was happening. When they finally opened their mouths, they stuck their collective feet in them, essentially telling him, "The only reason you're going through this is because obviously there's something you've done." So Job had to accept the fact that, "My wife cannot intercede for me. My friends cannot intercede for me. So I have to now stay in the presence of God and go forward on my own."

Job had to stay in God's presence to discern His will. Thankfully, he already had practice doing that. Scripture tells us that he would bring God sacrifices on behalf of his kids just in case they had sinned against Him. Job knew what his wife and friends did not understand. When we bring others to Jesus, we must learn to sit in His presence, even when it's the uncomfortable seat.

Now that you've learned how to pray pursuing these five disciplines, I want to make sure you understand what a life of prayer looks like. In part 3, we're going to talk about specific ways prayer can lead us to unshakable faith. We'll start with what happens when there's a communication breach. Have you ever felt as if you were praying to a wall? Read on, my friend. You're about to discover some important truths about you and God.

LET'S TALK

- Have you ever been the object of intercession? How did it feel to know someone was bringing you to Jesus?
- Have you felt the weight of a person's burdens when interceding for them?
- Do you find that sitting in that center seat can often be an uncomfortable place? Why or why not?
- Has your understanding of intercession changed after reading this chapter?
- Think about how you pray for others. Are you praying for your will to be done or God's?
- How will you pray for others differently going forward?

PART III

A LIFE OF PRAYER

Chapter 9

A COMMUNICATION BREACH

Why Is It Sometimes So Hard to Pray?

> Trust in the LORD with all your heart and do not lean on your own understanding. In all your ways acknowledge Him, and He will make your path straight.
>
> —PROVERBS 3:5–6, NASB

WHEN WE TALK about a prayer life that develops unshakable faith, we have to recognize that there will always be barriers—and we have to identify those roadblocks. I can tell you right now that the enemy doesn't want you praying. He also doesn't want you to identify the hindrances that may keep you from an active prayer life and seeing God's plans for your life come to fruition. What gets in the way of this intimacy, of us seeking the face of God? Let's take a deep dive and look at why prayer can be difficult sometimes and how in prayer we break through those barriers.

CONDITIONED *NOT* TO SEEK GOD

One of the former pastors in our church, Pastor Solomon, introduced me to a church leader from rural West Africa.

As I talked to this man who grew up on the other side of the world from me, I realized just how much we in the US have conditioned ourselves *not* to seek God.

The pastor shared with me, "When you get sick here in America, you run to the doctor because you have doctors; you have insurance. When we get sick, we have no choice but to run to God because our medical care is so lacking and expensive. When you want to buy a home, you go to the bank to get a loan. When we want a home, we go to God and pray for materials and people to help us build a home because there's no real bank to go to for a loan. We have no choice but to go to God and depend on Him for everything, for life."

He's right! We've been conditioned and enticed to run to what's accessible and available rather than to God. When was the last time you actually ran to God and waited for Him to move? So much around us is vying for our attention. Satan wants us to look for quick answers because he knows that quick answers keep us from going to God in prayer. Convenience keeps us from seeking God's face. Soon, we can't even make out God's voice because of all the static on the line.

Jeremiah 17 gives us a glimpse of those who are cursed and unhappy because they're trusting in themselves or in other people. They're struggling like a shrub in the desert or like the chaff the wind drives away.

> Cursed is the one who trusts in man, who draws strength from mere flesh and whose heart turns away from the LORD. That person will be like a bush in the wastelands; they will not see prosperity when

> it comes. They will dwell in the parched places of the desert, in a salt land where no one lives.
>
> —Jeremiah 17:5–6

To be honest with you, I have seen the church, or the body of Christ in America, make us lazy about going to God. Too many times, we would rather run to a prophet or to someone who can give us a word from God rather than go to God and get our word directly from Him. I've seen people put themselves in front of the veil that has been ripped and say, "Come to me, and I will tell you what God is saying. Come to me, and I will go to God for you." And I've seen thousands flock to people like that. All too often, we're guilty of running to men and women more quickly than to God. We tend to run to God as a last resort when all the human mechanisms we've relied on have failed.

> We've been conditioned and enticed to run to what's accessible and available rather than to God.

As a pastor, I often hear people say, "Pray for me, Pastor. God hears you." When they say that, I always tell them, "I won't pray *for* you; I will pray *with* you." I know that my assignment is to push people to the feet of God, not to pull them toward me. Every time I pray online, every time I lead corporate prayer, I'm showing people how they can go to Christ on their own. I believe God will move in your life as you, yourself, cultivate a life of prayer. That's what He did for me when I stopped leaning on Edward Christian and learned to pray on my own. And that's what He did for the Israelites. When God led them to Mount Sinai and told Moses to come up the mountain, He made sure the Israelites had a front-row seat to the conversation—that they were seeing, smelling, and breathing the smoke; hearing the thunder; and watching the fire. (Read it for yourself in Exodus 19.) The Lord made very sure they saw, heard, and felt His presence.

I believe that encounter sparked a desire in them to go to God on their own. God knew the only way His people would desire a relationship with Him was if they could witness it. He knew that years later, His people would tell their children, grandchildren, and great-grandchildren how they personally saw and experienced God—and that they would teach them to look for God and only Him.

The need for instant gratification tends to breach our conversation with God because we look to other things—like power, control, bank accounts, careers, material things, and even other people—to fulfill us. And those substitutions separate us from God. It's what happened when, thirteen chapters later in Exodus 32, the Israelites got tired of waiting for Moses to come down from the mountain. Complaining, they went to Moses' brother, Aaron, and said, "Come, make us gods who will go before us" (Exod. 32:1). So Aaron said, "Take off your gold earrings," and he melted them together and fashioned them into a golden calf—an idol to worship. (See Exodus 32:2–4.) They replaced God with, of all things, a cow.

And man, there were consequences! When Moses got down from the mountain, he melted down the calf, ground it into powder, and made the people drink it! And what did God do? He essentially told Moses, "Shift Me outside the camp, get Me out of the middle because they have breached the communication." So Moses ordered the Tent of Meeting, where God's presence dwelled, to be set up outside the camp. (See Numbers 2:17.)

Where have you moved God? What have you replaced Him with? What idols have you built and worshipped that tell God, "You're no longer in the center of my life and my heart"? My guess is that you haven't created anything as tangible as a golden calf. The idols in your life are probably much more subtle. But make no mistake, we have a ruthless and strategic enemy that's out to destroy our communication with God. That's because when we have no direct communication with Jesus—when we have no prayer—we have no relationship with Him.

C. S. Lewis says it well in *The Screwtape Letters*, a novel of letters from a senior demon named Screwtape, who teaches another demon named Wormwood their "work." Screwtape tells Wormwood, "It does not matter how small the sins are, provided that their cumulative effect is to edge the man away from the Light and out into the Nothing....Indeed the safest road to Hell is the gradual one—the gentle slope, soft underfoot, without sudden turnings, without milestones, without signposts."[1] To that list, I would add "without prayer."

Don't make the mistake of thinking Satan's going to leave your prayer life alone, that he's not going to try to interfere and stir up static on the line to the point that you just quit talking to God. That's exactly what he wants. It's why Paul writes in Ephesians 6 that we must guard our hearts from communication breaches by wearing the full armor of God that brings us to prayer. Look what Paul writes immediately after making that statement.

> And pray in the Spirit on all occasions with all kinds of prayers and requests. With this in mind, be alert and always keep on praying for all the Lord's people.
>
> —Ephesians 6:18

Pride's Trappings and Surrender's Power

Lately we've seen a high suicide rate among pastors. In the past few years, increasing numbers of church leaders have taken their lives. I'm sure you've heard these tragic stories. Maybe you've even known someone. Last year, an African American pastor I knew overdosed in his hotel room. He was on the rise, but he fell back into a previous drug addiction, which brought his end.

> Don't make the mistake of thinking Satan's going to leave your prayer life alone, that he's not going to try to interfere and stir up static on the line to the point that you just quit talking to God.

As a pastor, I can say that the spirit of pride was likely his ultimate demise. Church leaders don't want to be seen as broken. We don't want to be perceived as unable to cope with the pressures that come along with leading a church. We don't want to admit to ourselves or anyone else that we messed up and made a mistake. I've seen leaders put themselves on a pedestal they're not ready for yet or paint a picture of themselves that's not true. And then when they find out they're not as spiritual, deep, or anointed as they thought they were, their whole world comes crashing down.

Yet all of us struggle with the sin of pride, not just pastors. Every day, we confront our pride. For most of us, we are the star of our own movie, the main character in our story. We tend to think of ourselves more highly than we should and forget our place. That's why throughout Scripture, God warns against pride. In Romans 12:3, the apostle Paul says, "Do not think of yourself more highly than you ought." And Ezekiel 28:17 tells us straight-up that pride was the very sin of Satan: "your heart became proud on account of your beauty, and you corrupted your wisdom because of your splendor." God detests pride. He abhors it. He's a jealous God, and He wants us all to Himself. He knows—and this is key!—that our pride can be the very dagger that severs our communication with Him. He knows that our pride can end our prayer life and kill our relationship with God.

When we let our pride cut off our communication with God, any one of us can lose our bearings and make potentially fatal mistakes. I think of the prodigal son and how the Bible says he was lying among the pigs. In Luke 15:17, Jesus says, "And when he came to his senses…" This guy let his pride rob him of his senses. He went from a mansion to a pig trough, fighting for the slop of swine. He lost his mind.

When I think about David, I always remember that God called him "a man after my own heart" (Acts 13:22), because regardless of what they went through together, David would always humble himself in the presence of God. The Book of Psalms is written at various stages of David's life: broken stages, confused stages, fearful stages. But no matter what season he was in, David always ended up in the presence of God, surrendering his pride.

Do you remember what happened to King Nebuchadnezzar? He's another example of the power of surrender. We tend to think of him as the king of Babylonia who threw Shadrach, Meshach, and Abednego into the fiery furnace. But there is so much more to this ruler. God wanted so badly to reach Nebuchadnezzar that He sent Daniel and his friends to witness to him during their Babylonian exile. He sent an angel into the furnace and worked a miracle before Nebuchadnezzar's eyes. But the king still thought of himself as a god. It took destroying his pride by stripping away his authority, his kingdom, and even his mental faculties to bring the king to God.

> God knows that our pride can be the very dagger that severs our communication with Him and kills our relationship.

At one point, the king had a disturbing and confusing dream and asked Daniel to tell him what it meant. Everything Daniel interpreted in the king's dream came to pass. For years, Nebuchadnezzar ran through the woods, eating grass and living like the wild animals. In his letter in Daniel 4, Nebuchadnezzar said his hair "grew like the feathers of an eagle" and his nails "became like the claws of a bird" (Dan. 4:33). For seven long years, this man was brought to his lowest point. Nebuchadnezzar reigned from 605 BC to roughly 562 BC. Scholars point to a notable absence of any recorded major military operations led by Nebuchadnezzar for seven years, from 582 to 575 BC.[2] And then finally, after almost a decade of living like a madman, this former king who had literally been stripped of everything looked to God. He looked toward heaven, and his mind was restored. Finally, this former king recognized his place before his Creator, and this was his prayer:

> His dominion is an eternal dominion; his kingdom endures from generation to generation. All the peoples of the earth are regarded as nothing. He does as he pleases with the powers of heaven and the peoples of the earth. No one can hold back his hand or say to him: "What have you done?"
>
> —Daniel 4:34–36

Nebuchadnezzar had been broken, brought to his knees. He had surrendered his pride and now he had direct communication and relationship with God. We don't know the details of what happened in his remaining years, but we do know that God restored him to his throne. Nebuchadnezzar ended his letter saying, "Now I, Nebuchadnezzar, praise and exalt and glorify the King of heaven, because everything he does is right and all his ways are just. And those who walk in pride he is able to humble" (Dan. 4:37).

Where Shame and Guilt Thrive

If you're experiencing shame or guilt right now and you haven't prayed in a while (or maybe you've never prayed to the one true God), I'm talking to you. I want you to listen closely and ask the Holy Spirit to invade your thoughts and heart as you read this section, because I think you're missing one of the biggest truths about the promises and nature of our Creator and Savior.

Here it is. Are you ready? *Nothing, not one thing, you have done—and nothing that has been done to you—is so bad that you can't come back to God.* Nothing is so terrible that He would not hear you. If you don't get that, you're either not aware of, not understanding, or not accepting His work on the cross. You're missing that He is a loving and faithful God who is full of grace and waiting for you to fall at His feet and just pray.

Throughout my life, I've watched people walk away from God and quit the faith rather than pray. Some men have told me they thought they would never do certain things, and then they do. Think about Peter and his denial of Christ or Judas and his betrayal. Look at Elijah. When he gave in to depression, he left his servant and ran off by himself into a cave. What I've realized is that after a fall, people become like either Elijah, Judas, or Peter. The difference between these three men is that two ran off alone. Judas committed suicide, and Elijah quit. But Peter ran back to the disciples, and he went on to build the church.

Hear this and don't forget it: Alone is when the enemy gets to talk louder. Shame and guilt thrive in silence. There's true power in speaking your shame because you break the silence; you shine a light into the darkness. When David slept with Bathsheba, he did his best to hide his sin. Shame and guilt consumed him before Nathan confronted David and broke the silence. He shined a light on David's shame. Now David could go for broke, confess his sin, and return to God. In Psalm 51, David wrote, "Create in me a clean heart, O God, and renew a right spirit within me" (v. 10, ESV). But it took exposure to bring him to that place. It takes us acknowledging our shame to bring us back to Him. Restoration comes through being in our Savior's presence.

> Alone is when the enemy gets to talk louder.

You can *always* come back to the feet of God. Let me say that again. At any time and at any place, you can come back to God—no matter what you've done or what you've said. The question is, *How* do you return? You can't come in pride. You can't come making excuses, rationalizing your choices, or blaming someone else. You must come broken. In Ezekiel 16:6, God gave His prophet words for Jerusalem. He told Ezekiel to tell His people, "I…saw you kicking about in your blood." A person doesn't get much more broken than that. But pay attention to what happens next.

> I said to you, "Live!" I made you grow like a plant of the field and you grew and developed and entered puberty. Your breasts had formed and your hair had grown [I love the Bible], yet you were stark naked. Later I passed by, and when I looked at you and saw that you were old enough for love, I spread the corner of my garment over you and covered your naked body. I gave you my solemn oath and entered into a covenant with you, declares the Sovereign Lord, and you became *mine*.
>
> —Ezekiel 16:6–8, emphasis added

Wow! Do you get that? You are His. Paul says that *nothing* can separate you from Him—neither death nor life, neither angels nor demons, neither the present nor the future, nor any powers, neither height nor depth, nor anything else in all creation (Rom. 8:38). Whoa! That's so good! I resolved a long time ago that I wouldn't let anything lock me out of His presence. There may be times when I can't hold up my head, but I'll come in sackcloth and ashes and do whatever needs to be done to get back into His presence. Don't ever let shame and guilt keep you from coming to Him.

WHO'S IN YOUR VILLAGE?

We're all going to fall. None of us is exempt from falling or failing at some point in our lives. But we can be assured that when that happens, our relationship with God is still intact. It hasn't been eradicated. We can know for certain that we can always go to God in prayer. Scripture is clear about that truth.

> You can *always* come back to the feet of God. The question is, *How* do you return?

But I'm convinced it's essential to have a village around you—people who are on your side—who will also remind you that God is always there, especially in the difficult times of life—people who will raise you up, who will pray with you and intercede for you. Growing up, one of my pastors, a woman named Allie Trimuel, was part of my village. If I was going through something, I didn't even have to tell her. God would. If I was at a low point, before long I would get a call from her asking me what was going on. In the early years of my marriage, if Anna and I were going through something, I could call her and she would pray. She had great communication with both of us.

Today my village stretches to people outside my city, because as I've traveled in ministry, my village has expanded. But there are ten to twelve people in my church that I've identified to be part of my personal prayer village. I knew I needed a village that knew how to pray, and I knew each person in it had to speak the language of prayer. I prayed for God to give me discernment as I handpicked each one, and these individuals have amazing prayer lives. I met them in various small groups and have served with them on committees and outreaches our church leads. Some I met in our church's 4:00 a.m. prayer service. I never brought them up in front of the church or put a spotlight on them. I privately called all of them into a room—they didn't really know the purpose of the meeting—and gave each one a picture of me in a frame. I also handed them a necktie I had worn and told them, "You have the responsibility to hold this picture and this necktie and pray for me." I told them, "Your responsibility is to consistently cover me. Grab this picture, grab this tie, and go to prayer."

I call them my secret snipers, because nobody knows who they are. And they are shooting down the enemy. I've told them, "Anytime you see me in a low place or if you think I look tired, your responsibility is to grab that picture and that fabric and pray." Sometimes I get on my knees before them and ask them to stretch their hands toward me in prayer. Every now and then I'll call them, I'll see them, or I'll text them and ask, "You still have my picture, right?"

Jesus was intentional about building His village. He even brought close friends to pray with Him in the Garden of Gethsemane. Everyone needs a village. God created us for relationship with Him as well as with others. It's literally why we're breathing. You and I were created to need someone. It is in us. God looked at Adam and said, "It is not good that man should be alone" (Gen. 2:18, NKJV). We all need someone to be there for us. The worst thing you can do is think you can do this life alone. We need others lifting us up to help us push through the barriers when prayer is difficult.

Our village can be a lifeline. In Acts 14, we read about when Paul was stoned in Lystra. Scripture says the crowd dragged him outside the city, thinking he was dead. But after the disciples gathered around Paul and prayed, he got up and went right back into the city. His village got around him. You need a village that will gather with you and pray.

This is where prayer comes in big time! Pray for discernment to help you identify people you can call on for prayer and ask God to begin to prepare their hearts. You can do like I did and gather everyone together; or you can privately go to each one and ask them to be part of your prayer village. Don't make it difficult or complex. You can ask for prayer and let them know you'll be part of their prayer village.

As a church leader whose life is always under the microscope, I'll be the first to say that allowing people to get that emotionally and spiritually close to me wasn't easy. But as I prayed, God made it clear that I needed others in my life praying for me. So I asked Him for courage and discernment to invite the right people into my life: "God, I'm following Your instruction in obedience. But You know that this is really hard for me. You know that I'm hesitant to let people get this close. Will You show me who should be part of my prayer village, and will You begin to prepare their hearts and my heart for this conversation? Will You help me to be transparent and open my heart to what You have for me through these relationships?"

> We need others lifting us up to help us push through the barriers when prayer is difficult.

If you're afraid to let people in, talk to God. Bring your fears to Him and ask Him to begin to work in your life. It may be that gathering a group like this won't be an immediate action step. Maybe you'll need to wrap this petition in prayer and give God room to bring this to fruition in His own time. Don't rush it. Start to pray about it and ask God to show you the next steps.

Staying Broken Before God

That doesn't sound like a lot of fun, right? How many of us want to "stay broken"? Does God really call us to remain broken before Him throughout our lives? As I've said, my go-to is always Scripture. Let's look at what God's Word says. In Proverbs 3:5–6 (NASB), we're told how to protect our relationship with God:

> Trust in the LORD with all your heart and do not lean on your own understanding. In all your ways acknowledge Him, and He will make your paths straight.

This is one of my favorite passages in the Bible because it shows us what our position should be throughout our life. And don't miss the promise in it either. God is telling us, "In all your ways, communicate with Me, keep Me in the center, and I'll show you how to navigate through the different and even difficult seasons of your life. But never think you can do it without acknowledging Me. Never think you can do it on your own."

That's what He means when He says, "Do not lean on your own understanding." You are totally, totally, totally dependent on Him (and yes, I meant to say that three times because I want you to understand your position). That's a very humbling and broken place. Regardless of your social status, your success, your role in your church; regardless of who validates you; regardless even of your spiritual maturity, always understand that there's no good thing in your flesh. Never lean on your understanding, and always stay broken before God, because every season of life brings another battle, another challenge.

The challenges that I had in my twenties weren't the challenges I had in my thirties. And the trials I encountered in my thirties were different from those in my forties. Certain things I would run to God about then aren't even issues for me now. But certain things that I didn't worry about in my twenties are now an issue. Now that I'm in my fifties, my eyesight is changing. Sometimes I get up and I grab my hands because my joints are hurting. At the onset of COVID-19, the older people were most susceptible to the virus while the younger people walked around without face masks and unconcerned. As we get older, our challenges change. We start praying about our future and retirement. In all your ways, in every area and every inch of your life, acknowledge Him.

At the same time, our communication with God and others also changes with our challenges. Every relationship you have involves some form of communication. You communicate with your children differently as they get older. If you're married, you probably communicate differently with your spouse than when you started dating. You communicate differently with a friend you've had for decades versus someone you just met. When there is no communication, you begin to feel the gap and ask, "What's going on here?" That's because the relationship is not what it used to be. A parent can always tell when their child is growing older because the communication changes. We have to be careful that no matter how old we grow in Christ, we protect the communication and remain dependent on Him. There is no age limit on Acts 17:28: "In Him we live and move and have our being" (NKJV).

This truth applies throughout our lives—from when we're just starting out all the way to when our life on this earth is ending. When we stay broken before God, dependent on Him, we recognize our need for prayer. Through prayer, we get to walk with our Savior, talking to Him, listening to Him, and experiencing life with Him as our faith grows unshakable. And we get to do that through every season for the rest of our lives—until we're with Him face to face.

I love that picture of walking with Jesus through life. But those paths will not be only straight and smooth. The older we get, the more we realize we need to persevere in prayer despite what we do or don't see. Not sure what that means? Read on.

Let's Talk

- When has it been hard for you to pray? What was causing the communication breach?
- Have you replaced God in your life at times? If so, how? If not, how did you avoid it?

- Has pride ever interfered in your prayer life? Please explain your response.
- When you think about being broken before God, how does that make you feel? (Be honest.)
- If you're walking through shame and guilt right now, take a minute to tell God about it and be specific. Go back and read this chapter and be reminded that you are His.

Chapter 10

THE STRETCH

Why Must We Persevere in Prayer?

Then Jesus told his disciples a parable to show them that they should always pray and not give up.
—Luke 18:1

It was the Shunammite mother's darkest hour. The young son she had prayed for in her old age was suddenly dead. But she had been kind to a man of God over the years, even built him a room in her home where he could stay whenever he came to town. So before she told anyone else what happened, she ran to tell the prophet Elisha, believing he could raise her son.

As soon as the woman told the prophet her son was dead, Elisha gave his staff to his servant Gehazi and told him to run to the woman's home and lay it on the boy's face. Even though Gehazi was headed to her home, the grieving mother refused to leave Elisha's side, and the two headed to her home. Along the way, they met up with Gehazi, who told them he had followed Elisha's commands, but nothing happened.

When Elisha arrived at the woman's home, he went into the room where the boy lay, shut the door, and prayed. But still nothing happened. Then Elisha got up and stretched his body over the lifeless child. We're talking eye to eye, nose to nose, mouth to mouth, hands to hands. It's an awkward yet powerful scene. Stretched out over the boy, Elisha felt the child's body grow warm. Then Elisha walked back and forth in the room before again stretching his body over the boy. Second Kings 4:35 tells us the boy sneezed seven times and opened his eyes.

This story paints a picture of perseverance, which was demonstrated by both the mother and Elisha, God's prophet. Let's look at Elisha's steps. First, he sent Gehazi to lay his staff on the boy. Nothing happened, but Elisha continued to walk to the house. He was persevering. Then he continued to press as he walked in the room and shut the door. He prayed, and again nothing happened. But still, he pushed. He laid on the boy, but his lifeless body only got warm. He pushed again. Then he got on the bed and stretched out on the boy a second time. Finally, life!

The question is, "When would *you* have stopped?" Would you have stopped the moment the mother came to you with the news that her son had died? Would you have stopped the moment Gehazi told you nothing happened? Would you have stopped when you prayed one time? Would you have stopped when you lay down on the bed and the boy's body got warm? Would you have stopped when you paced in the room and nothing changed?

Too often we say, "I prayed about it," which, in truth, usually means we've prayed one time. But more often than not, perseverance in prayer is about stretching ourselves over and over. Perseverance is continued prayer, continued communication, regardless of what we see or hear. Despite seeing his daughter dying and even when he heard that she had died, Jairus persevered. He was stretched.

Hannah, the mother of Samuel, was stretched in all areas: spiritually, emotionally, mentally, and physically. For years Hannah prayed for a child. Scripture says that every year her husband, who loved her, made sacrifices, possibly pleading with God to open Hannah's womb. But nothing changed, and Hannah continued to be taunted and ridiculed by her husband's other wife, Peninnah. Weary and beaten down, one day Hannah took drastic action. She went to the temple and, in deep anguish, she prayed for a child.

> LORD Almighty, if you will only look on your servant's misery and remember me, and not forget your servant but give her a son, then I will give him to the LORD for all the days of his life.
>
> —1 SAMUEL 1:11

As she continued to pray, Eli the priest accused her of being drunk because her lips were moving yet no sound was coming out. But Hannah told the priest, "I was pouring out my soul to the LORD....I have been praying here out of my great anguish and grief" (1 Sam. 1:15–16).

Years of perseverance and probably thousands of personal prayers finally yielded an answer. Hannah conceived and gave birth to Samuel, whose name means, "Because I asked the LORD for him" (1 Sam. 1:20).

When I hear the word *persevere*, the word *push* always comes to mind. I grew up hearing that push was an acrostic for "Pray Until Something Happens." It makes me think about the parable Jesus told in Luke 18 about the widow who continued to go to the unjust judge, asking him to "grant me justice against my adversary" (v. 3). Several times he refused. But finally, he gave in because she kept pushing. She kept going to him with the same request until she wore him down. This widow shows us it's OK to push—that it's not only OK, but perseverance is also rewarded.

Perseverance is continuing in prayer regardless of what we see or hear.

Please don't fall into the trap of thinking that praying about something consistently means you don't have faith. That's a lie straight from the pit of hell. Scripture flat-out tells us to persevere in prayer. At the beginning of the parable about the woman and the unjust judge, Luke explained the point of the story. Look at what Jesus Himself said about His intention: "Then Jesus told his disciples a parable to show them that they should always pray and not give up.…And will not God bring about justice for his chosen ones, who cry out to him day and night? Will he keep putting them off? I tell you, he will see that they get justice, and quickly" (Luke 18:1, 7–8).

SIGNS OF CHANGE

As we persevere in prayer, often God gives us signs of movement like He did for Elisha. The boy grew warm. He wasn't alive, just warm. That's a sign, a message to keep us pushing and stretching, persevering even more and looking for additional signs of change.

One of my favorite examples of seeing signs of movement while persevering is found in 1 Kings 18. Israel was in a deep famine. No rain had fallen in years, and the earth was parched, and the crops had all withered and died. In the third year of the famine, God told Elijah that He was going to send rain on the land. Confident in God's promise, Elijah told King Ahab, "Go, eat and drink, for there is the sound of a heavy rain" (1 Kings 18:41). That's when Elijah climbed to the top of a mountain, bent down toward the ground with his face between his knees, and just prayed. Next, Elijah ordered Ahab's servant, who passionately followed God, to look for any signs of rain. "There is nothing there," he told Elijah. But just because the servant didn't see anything doesn't mean Elijah stopped praying.

He continued to persevere. Seven times he told the servant to go back and look toward the sea. Talk about persevering! The seventh time, the servant returned, saying, "You know, I do see a cloud but what I see doesn't look like abundance. It's only the size of a man's hand." (See 1 Kings 18:44.) At first, he saw nothing, but now he saw something, and that was enough to motivate Elijah to keep praying. Finally, the sky grew dark with clouds, and the rain poured down. The sign you see or hear may not be the "abundance of rain" you're praying for, but it's more than what you saw before. Any glimpse of hope is a sign that God is moving.

I think of the people of Sudan, especially the almost two million Christians who live there today. For thirty long years, the Sudanese people lived under strict Islamic Sharia law rigidly enforced by the cruel anti-Christian dictator Omar al-Bashir. If you remember the genocide and crimes against humanity that took place in Darfur in the early 2000s, Bashir was the ruler behind these atrocities. He was behind the unjust killing and mistreatment of thousands of people.[1] You can imagine the kind of terror anyone who left Islam for another religion faced under his reign. Christians in Sudan have told chilling stories of the stonings, torture, and vile attacks they endured because of their faith.

> Any glimpse of hope is a sign that God is moving.

I'm sure that throughout three decades of tyranny in Sudan, millions of prayers have gone up for the Sudanese people. In 2018, the fruit of that perseverance began to sprout as small signs of change surfaced. Suffering under a failing economy and ever-worsening living conditions, Sudan's citizens began to raise their voices in small ways. Then more signs of change came as protests against Bashir and his regime erupted in the streets.

In April 2019, Bashir was ousted and a transitional government came into power. It was a huge sign that God was moving and motivation to keep praying. A little over a year later, in July 2020, the Sudanese government abolished the death penalty for leaving Islam. Then three months later, in September, the country that had suffered so intensely took a historic step and put an end to hardline Sharia law, which called for such vile acts as female genital mutilation and the death penalty for leaving Islam. The pictures of Sudanese men and women dancing in the streets are beautiful—the result of thirty years of perseverance in prayer!

We can see similar signs of change in the Hebrews' deliverance from Egypt into the Promised Land of Canaan. God gave them so many indicators: the plagues, the Passover, the parting of the Red Sea. There were so many signs that He had heard their cries and was about to move mightily. I realize that you may have been praying for years for something to happen, for God to move and bring change in your life or another's. But don't forget to look for the signs of movement—even if they're only the size of a man's hand.

God's Doing Something

As a pastor, I've heard some pretty crazy ideas and questions. I've had people tell me, "Well, God knows the need, Pastor. He knows my request. Why do I have to continue to pray?" Simple. He tells us to. He tells us to persevere because in our persistence we are changed. As we stretch, yes, there's usually pain involved, but there's also great benefit.

One of the biggest things that has stretched me is pastoring. Every year for ten years I would go to Phoenix, Arizona, to a conference led by Pastor Tommy Barnett. And every year, I would climb his Prayer Mountain. It's a twenty-four-hour prayer pavilion Tommy's son built for his dad on the side of a mountain behind the church. Each time when I got to the top, I wrote down my petitions on a piece of paper and left that paper on the mountain. With some things, I'd get immediate answers. But there were some petitions that required more time. So I'd climb the mountain again the next year and again leave my handwritten petitions.

Before our church had a permanent building, we were holding services in a high school auditorium that seated seven hundred. Every Sunday, we held three services. Every Sunday at every service, someone accepted the Lord (it's still happening today). Someone came to the Lord every Sunday. You can't get those kinds of results without prayer. The school began to see our crowds increase, and they started to demand more money. I remember climbing that prayer mountain and telling the Lord, "God, we need our own place."

> Jesus tells us to persevere because in our persistence we are changed.

But the stretch was more than just needing a building. It was also getting the finances and waiting for the right piece of land to become available. I'll never forget it. One of our goals was to save one million dollars. The moment we saved a million dollars, a church building became available. We paid for it with cash. It was almost like God was telling me, "OK, you have climbed this mountain for three years, but while you were climbing, I was blessing you and you were saving. While you were climbing, I was basically making the land available for you." He monitored my faithfulness, my consistency, my perseverance, and my stretch. Every year, I hid my petition in the mountain: "We need our church. We need our church." During that time, God matured my faith. It took faith to return to that mountain and climb it over and over. It took faith to keep saving money. Each time, it stretched my trust in God.

Part of that stretch was staying consistent in my climb but also in my petition. One of the things you have to be careful of is not changing your petition. Each time I climbed, I prayed the exact same thing. I didn't ask, "Give me another place to rent." I said, "We need our own place. Give us our own space." After we bought the first building, I walked down the street where it sat, and I noticed another smaller church on another block with a "for sale" sign out front. We called and inquired about the building, but it was under contract. So I prayed, "God, we need this building too. I need that contract to fail." We paid cash for that building also. Then I looked across the street and saw another building for sale. We bought that one as well.

Overall, we wound up purchasing four blocks of buildings, including forty-four pieces of property, and paid cash for each one. I remember when we bought the first building. It seated only eleven hundred. Some members of our church board questioned me, "Why would you buy a building we can barely fit into?" Imagine if I had given in to the pressure and not bought it. We didn't know at the time that once we bought that building, God was going to give us more property around the corner. But we couldn't have started the process of buying all those other buildings until we bought the first one.

We're in the heart of a Chicago community surrounded by poverty. There were people living in the houses near the ones we bought, and they started coming to the church asking, "Do you want to buy my house?" The story behind how we acquired every piece of land we purchased and how we paid cash for each one is amazing. The growth plan that unfolded for our church wasn't just a good idea; it was a God thing. The main building has four thousand seats, and we didn't build it as a church. It's a performing arts center because the goal is to bring the arts back to the urban community. Then we bought a factory, three levels high, across the street that we turned into a children's center. You can't have those kinds of results without prayer. This happened because of a consistent climb, a consistent stretch, and a consistent petition.

In chapter 2, I shared that my mother was diagnosed

with cancer. I remember praying, "I believe; I believe; I believe; I believe." Seven months later, I was burying her. Losing her rocked my entire world. But I persevered. I'm still here. I never left God. Her death was one of the toughest things for me to accept. But as I persisted for my mother's life, the Lord worked in my prayer life. Sometimes we just don't realize that in our persistence God is doing something powerful.

PERSEVERING EVEN WHEN YOU DON'T GET WHAT YOU WANT

OK, this is good. Are you ready? I have learned so much from David. In 2 Samuel 12, when Nathan went to him and exposed David's sin, he also told him that the child he conceived with Bathsheba was going to die. Immediately, David flung himself on the altar and prayed. He was praying, praying, praying and asking God to please turn the situation around. He fasted and didn't sleep. Instead, he stayed on the ground all night, praying. He was right there with God. That went on for seven days. The whole time, David was pushing and pushing. On the seventh day, he looked up and learned that the child was dead.

Then David did the unexpected. He got up, washed himself, put on some lotion, changed his clothes, and headed into the temple to worship. After that, he went home and got something to eat. His servants couldn't believe what they were seeing: "Bro, how can you just jump up from all that fasting and prayer and start eating?" It's because in prayer, David realized that the situation was in the Lord's hands. He said to his servants, "I can continue to pray and fast, but it's not going to bring the baby back." (See 2

Samuel 12:22–23.) Persevering in prayer prepares you for whatever results you get. Sometimes, even when you persevere, God doesn't give you what you asked for, but He will condition your heart to His will.

Like many couples, my wife, Anna, and I desired to have children. Together, we prayed for a child. We consulted with doctors and specialists. We did everything that couples who desperately want children do. At one point, though, Anna was told that if she tried certain procedures or took certain drugs, there could be side effects. This was thirty years ago; technology is different now. Anna, who is a nurse, looked at me and said, "I feel we are taking control out of God's hand." That's when we made a conscious decision to pray that God's will would be done.

How do you pray out of what you want and into what He wants? That was the battle in the Garden of Gethsemane when Christ prayed, "If there's any other way, take this cup from Me." But eventually He said, "Not My will but Yours be done." (See Matthew 26:39 and Luke 22:42.) Years later, Anna and I were able to say to ourselves, "Now we see. Now we understand what God was up to." I don't have any natural children, but I father so many in the spiritual realm. Anna has mentored women and girls. We've both poured into more vessels outside the house than we could have ever birthed in the house.

But it has been a long, sometimes difficult road to walk. I remember when we were at the age when all our friends were having kids. If I found out someone was pregnant, I didn't share it with Anna because I didn't know where it would take her. I didn't realize that she had already tapped into "not our will, but His will." As a pastor, I have to christen and bless babies. I have to bless what God didn't let me have. There's a place in prayer you must go to where you trust that even if He doesn't give you your desire, He's still God. I'm telling you firsthand: You can't get to that place of deep surrender unless you tap into His will through continued prayer. There are some things you could make happen, but then you will have entered the permissive will of God and not the perfect will of God. (Go back and read chapter 8 on intercession, where we took a deep dive into perfect and permissive will.)

> I'm telling you firsthand: You can't get to that place of deep surrender unless you tap into His will through continued prayer.

I was taught that God always answers prayer, and His answer is yes, no, or wait. The hardest part for Anna and me—and this is being very open and honest—stemmed from the people who were praying for us to have kids. There were even those who would come to us with a "prophetic word." Even though we'd accepted His will, others kept coming in, trying to force another will on us. Once you accept God's will, there will always be those people, those enemies, those "friends of Job," who make it difficult to continue loving His will over your desire. That's why we have to persevere in prayer, because prayer prepares us for whatever the answer is.

That's another reason God has given us prayer, right? He knows that this world is trouble. Jesus blatantly tells us that in John 16:33: "I have told you these things, so that in me you may have peace. In this world you will have trouble. But take heart! I have overcome the world." Trouble is the result of living on the earth. A life of prayer readies us for those things. It builds unshakable faith.

I'll never forget an episode of *The Oprah Winfrey Show* that featured a woman who wanted a kid so desperately she made it happen, and the baby was born with special needs. She said, "I made it happen, but parenting is not what I thought it would be. It's demanding more out of me. Now I'm mad. I got what I wanted, but it didn't happen the way I dreamed." It's best to persevere, praying into His will, no matter how hard it is. Yes, it's a battle.

Everyone needs to give themselves time in prayer to grow in His will. To me, two of the most powerful words in prayer are, "Yes, Lord." That's because saying, "Yes, Lord," means I accept Him over myself. I accept His will over mine. And please remember, "Yes, Lord" is not a one-time prayer but one we must pray each and every day.

When you accept His will, you take God off probation. When I worked in law enforcement, I saw the limitations that probation put on a person—all because they had not quite proved themselves as trustworthy or responsible. They had a curfew. Their whereabouts were monitored. They had certain "house rules" they had to adhere to. Their lives were full of contingencies and conditions. When we take God off probation, we drop all contingencies and follow Him unconditionally, regardless of what may or may not happen in our life.

Contentment, insight, and transcending peace don't come overnight. They don't come from just one prayer.

Many times when we don't get what we want, we bring charges against God. I can tell you right now that this affects your prayer life. You can't call Him holy (which means perfect) if you're holding something against Him. And if you haven't allowed Him to be perfect in your life, it puts static on the line. It affects how you go before the throne, and it reveals who God is to you. If you see God as a genie who is supposed to grant your wish, you'll get mad at Him when you don't get what you want. But when you unconditionally accept His will, you drop any and all charges you may have against Him. You release Him from probation by asking Him to be Lord over your life. I learned that in prayer.

WHEN SILENCE PERVADES, PRAY ANYWAY

What happens when you pray and don't hear anything? When the silence is deafening? I would say this is when learning how to persevere in prayer is the most important. If you think about Joseph in the Old Testament, he had to contend with extreme isolation and silence. We know that God spoke to Joseph in two dreams about his destiny when he was a young man. But we never read when Joseph dreamed again. We never read that he dreamed when his brothers threw him into the pit or when he was sold into slavery. Scripture never tells us he dreamed or heard God speak to him when he was in prison. All we see is a sustained period of silence during which Joseph had to hold on to what he heard in those early dreams. He was only seventeen when he was sold into slavery, and he didn't step into the reality of his dreams until he was thirty. God may show you your destiny, but He never gives you the roadmap. Instead, He compels you to trust and depend on Him and call out to Him. He makes you persevere.

> Contentment, insight, and transcending peace don't come overnight. They don't come from just one prayer.

In the silence, God was perfecting Joseph. He was sharpening him for the right time to be called out. After interpreting the cupbearer's dream in prison, Joseph said to him, "When you get out of here, don't forget about me." (See Genesis 40:14.) But the cupbearer didn't remember him. Joseph remained in prison two more horrific years until finally he was called out to interpret Pharaoh's dream and ultimately was released from prison. What had God been doing in him in those two years? We don't know, but we do know that Joseph was praying the whole time. Otherwise, he would not have been ready when he was called out to become Pharaoh's right-hand guy, ruling over Egypt and eventually forgiving his brothers. In the silence and isolation, God was changing Joseph and transforming his heart.

> When you unconditionally accept His will, you drop any and all charges you may have against Him.

Psalm 1 says the person who does not stand in the counsel of the wicked or stand in the way of sinners or sit in the seat of the scornful is not only blessed. He or she is "like a tree planted by streams of water, which yields its fruit in season and whose leaf does not wither—whatever they do prospers" (v. 3). Whenever I think about that psalm, I always think about the fact that because the tree is planted by the water, it can stand firm even during a drought or a flood.

Cultivating a mature, persevering prayer life now prepares us for those times when we may not hear from God. Consistently spending time with Him enables us to be assured that we're actually part of Him, and He is part of us. We are connected—grafted into Him (John 15). If He's not saying anything, He will bring you to a place of His peace. I have to believe that supernatural peace is what got Joseph through all of the trials, silence, and deception he endured.

> God may show you your destiny, but He never gives you the roadmap.

When we let the silence overcome us and we fail to pray, we hit dead ends. Abraham shows us that. In Genesis 12:7, the Lord appeared to Abraham and said, "To your offspring, I will give this land." Abraham built an altar in Bethel. Then in verse 10, we learn there's a famine in the land. Trouble has come, but Abraham doesn't pray. Instead, he takes everything into his own hands. He and his wife, Sarah, travel to Egypt to look for food, and they tell one lie after another. Abraham says Sarah is his sister, and when he's exposed, Pharaoh orders him out. Abraham is forced to make a U-turn and return where? Back to Bethel—the place where he started, square one. (See Genesis 13:1–4.)

> Cultivating a mature, persevering prayer life now prepares us for those times when we may not hear from God.

When we don't seek the Lord for both overall and specific directions, we take matters into our own hands. At that point, when we're making decisions, we're compromising and hurting others. Abraham lied and had Sarah lie. He put his family in danger and hurt his wife—and he kept this up until finally he was evicted.

Sometimes without prayer, we hit dead-end roads and have to make a U-turn. We end up right back at square one. The moment I pull away and stop communicating with God, when I stop depending on Him and trusting Him, I'm on my own—trusting, depending on, and relying on myself. And if you don't know it by now, relying on yourself will always get you in trouble. In Romans 7:18, the apostle Paul says that "nothing good dwells in me, that is, in my flesh. For I have the desire to do what is right, but not the ability to carry it out" (ESV).

There are too many times in all of our lives that we could point to when we prayed about something and didn't see anything. We didn't hear anything. We didn't feel anything. But our Creator and Savior asks us to continue to pray and be in relationship with Him. Please, I beg you. If you're in a season of silence right now, don't believe the lie that you're a second-class Christian or that God is punishing you. God is silent for a reason. He may not be speaking, but you can take comfort in the fact that He *is* working, just as He was working in Joseph's life. The question is, Will you continue to pray in the silence? Will you continue to allow God to work in your heart?

> God is silent for a reason. He may not be speaking, but He *is* always working.

When the silence is surrounding you, recognize that you're not alone. Although God may seem silent, He's still working in you through your prayers. Don't doubt Him, and don't stop praying. He's inviting you to push forward and persevere. And praise God we don't have to do it alone. Read on to discover why gathering for prayer is so critical to a prayer life that withstands trials and even silence.

LET'S TALK

- Think of a time when you persevered in prayer. What did you learn about God? What did you learn about yourself?
- When do you find it difficult to persevere in prayer?
- Think about something you prayed for. What were the signs of movement leading up to your receiving the answer?
- What has God taught you about how He works through you when you persevere?
- Have you experienced times when God worked through silence? If so, how did the Lord use that season? If not, do you believe God can work through silence?

Chapter 11

THE SOUND

Why Do We Need to Pray With Others?

About midnight Paul and Silas were praying and singing hymns to God, and the other prisoners were listening to them. Suddenly there was such a violent earthquake that the foundations of the prison were shaken.
—Acts 16:25–26

"Holy, Holy, Holy is the Lord God Almighty, who was and is and is to come!" Day and night, the four winged beasts flock to the One seated on the throne. Flying back and forth, they ceaselessly cry out the words that have awed generations of believers through the ages. As their praise echoes through the heavens, the twenty-four elders cast their crowns before the throne, saying, "You are worthy, our Lord and God, to receive glory and honor and power, for you created all things, and by your will they were created and have their being" (Rev. 4:8, 11).

Can you picture John's vision of heaven captured in Revelation 4? Better question: Can you *hear* it? Can you hear the corporate sound, the thundering voices adoring and praising God? These are the endless sounds released through the heavenly realm. This is the sound our Lord sits in—the sound He continuously basks in. This is what He's accustomed to. So why wouldn't we as believers pray and release a symphony of sound that's pleasing to His ears?

As I began to write this chapter and started exploring Scripture, I found numerous places where sound is key to God moving. The sound we raise is an indicator of His power and faithfulness. It's no wonder our voices in prayer and worship are so attractive to Him.

THE POWER OF A SOUND

Throughout Scripture we see the power of the sound of prayer and praise and how they get God's attention.

The sound of victory

The ironclad walls of Jericho came crumbling down because of a sound. In Joshua 6, God told Joshua to have his troops march around the city for six days and to position seven priests carrying trumpets made of rams' horns in front of the ark of the covenant. On the seventh day, the sound of victory was released as the priests blew their trumpets. Upon hearing the long trumpet blast, the army gave a loud shout, and the thick walls thought to be so secure came tumbling down. The shout that God orchestrated brought down the city. God can use the sound of your shout to break through impenetrable barriers too.

The sound of a bold petition

In 2 Kings 20, when the prophet told King Hezekiah, "Get your house in order, you're going to die," the Judean king turned his face toward the wall and did two things: he cried out to God, and he begged Him for more time. As a result, God told the prophet, "Go back and tell Hezekiah I have heard your prayer and I have seen your tears and as a result of that, I will heal you." (See 2 Kings 20:5.) The sound of Hezekiah's bold petition bounced from the wall to heaven, and God responded by allowing him to live for fifteen more years.

The sound of rejoicing in God's presence

In 1 Samuel 4, the Israelites raised such a loud shout of joy upon seeing the ark of the covenant back in their midst that the earth literally shook. The Philistine army that had recently defeated Israel in battle heard the shouting and became fearful. They concluded, "Their God must be among them. We're lost....Who can save us from those powerful gods?" (See verses 7 and 8.) The sound of the people rejoicing over God's presence told their enemy that Israel's God was in their midst, and they knew they didn't stand a chance against Him. Guess what, your enemy knows he doesn't stand a chance against the almighty God. He just hopes you never realize that. Send up a sound that welcomes God's presence, and you'll see your enemy flee too.

The sound of a cry from the belly of hell

When Jonah was swallowed by the big fish, he cried out to the Lord: "And he heard me; out of the belly of hell I cried, and thou heardest my voice" (Jon. 2:2, KJV). In the belly of a fish—in the midst of a situation he shouldn't have been in and shouldn't have survived—Jonah released a sound that got God's attention. That tells me that no matter what situation I find myself in—I could even find myself facing what feels like hell on earth—if I lift up my voice to God, He will hear my cry.

The sound of unity

In Acts 1, after Jesus ascended to heaven, the eleven disciples gathered once again in the Upper Room where they were staying. Scripture tells us they all "joined together constantly in prayer" (v. 14). They had walked through so much together. And now there they were without the Master they had followed for three years. The sound of continuous, corporate prayer must have been incredibly comforting to the disciples as they followed Jesus' final instruction to wait for the Holy Spirit. And God responded to their sound by filling them with His Spirit and empowering them to do great exploits in His name. Our church has seen the power of this sound more times than I can count. God moves powerfully when His people release the sound of united prayer.

The sound of urgency

Bartimaeus, the blind beggar in Mark 10:46, got Jesus' attention by shouting His name: "Jesus, Son of David, have mercy on me!" Scripture says the crowd rebuked him, but that didn't stop Bartimaeus from releasing the sound. He shouted all the more, getting louder and louder: "Son of David, have mercy on me!" He cried out until Jesus stopped and said, "Call him." The sound drew Jesus to a man with no sight, and He healed him. Take that in for a minute. The man who had been blind could suddenly see—all because he opened his mouth and released a sound that got Jesus' attention. What miracle is waiting for you on the other side of the sound of your urgent plea?

The sound of desperation

The ten lepers in Luke 17 who braved the massive crowds to see Jesus realized quickly they would need to cry out to get His attention. They stood at a distance and called out in a loud voice, "Jesus, Master, have pity on us!" Jesus turned toward the sound, and they too were healed.

The sound of faithful praise

I often preach from Acts 16. At midnight, Paul and Silas were in jail, but they weren't sleeping. Instead, they were praying corporately and singing loudly—so loudly that the other prisoners were listening to them. In verse 25, the sound erupted, and suddenly there was a violent earthquake caused by the sound of praise that opened the prison doors and broke their chains. You've probably heard this before, but it's true: breakthrough and deliverance are on the other side of your sound of praise.

The sound of our prayers and praise causes foundations to be shaken, doors to be opened, and chains to be broken. And when we release our voices together in prayer, hold on, because God cannot ignore the sound. Jesus told us in Matthew 18:20 that where two or three are gathered together in His name, He will be in the midst of them. That was a powerful promise.

Getting God's Attention

The sound of your prayers and praise is an attention-getter. When you lift your voice, you compel God to look your way. Our Lord is attracted to the sound of our worship and intercession. Exodus 2:24 says God heard the groaning of the Israelites and remembered His covenant with Abraham, Isaac, and Jacob. Then verse 25 says, "God looked on the Israelites and was concerned about them." The New Living Translation says, "He...knew it was time to act."

> The sound of our prayers and praise causes foundations to be shaken, doors to be opened, and chains to be broken.

God is moved when we raise our voices to Him. But I'm comforted by the fact that God also hears our indiscernible groans and wailing, our deep cries. In his letter to the Romans, the apostle Paul shared this hopeful promise:

> In the same way, the Spirit helps us in our weakness. We do not know what we ought to pray for, but the Spirit himself intercedes for us through wordless groans. And he who searches our hearts knows the mind of the Spirit, because the Spirit intercedes for God's people in accordance with the will of God.
>
> —ROMANS 8:26–27

The Holy Spirit interprets our sound even when we can't or don't know how to pray. God hears even the faintest cry.

That brings me to an important point. It's critical that you understand we're releasing the sound of *prayer*, not the sound of *complaint*. When the children of Israel had no food in the wilderness, they didn't cry out to God for food. They *complained* about not having food. And when they didn't have water, they didn't cry out for water. They complained about the lack of water. One grumble after another. Actually, it was kind of a stockpile of complaints rather than a pile of prayer requests. Not only did they complain, they also began to hurl accusations at God and speak negative words about their destiny: "Did You bring us out here to die of thirst? We are going to die."

We have to monitor our sound. There is a blatant difference between a complaint and a request. The Israelites didn't request food or water. I want to mention Numbers 14:26–28—and this is key for really monitoring our confessions and prayer lives. In verse 26, the Lord said to Moses and Aaron, "How long will this wicked community grumble against me?" OK, now pay attention here because I want you to get this: God doesn't interpret their sound as prayer, but *He does still hear them*. He says, "I have heard the complaints of these grumbling Israelites. So tell them, 'As surely as I live, declares the Lord, I will do to you the very thing I heard you say'" (Num. 14:27–28). Remember, their complaining turned to accusing and even declaring their destiny: "We are going to die." Because God gave them what He heard them say, a whole generation died in the wilderness. Essentially, He told them, "You will never make it to the Promised Land because you did not pray; you grumbled."

We're releasing the sound of *prayer*, not the sound of *complaint*.

Have you ever read Revelation 8:3? As John continued to share his vision of heaven, the exiled prisoner on the Island of Patmos wrote, "Another angel, who had a golden censer, came and stood at the altar. He was given much incense to offer, with the prayers of all God's people, on the golden altar in front of the throne." The smoke of the incense, together with the prayers of God's people, go up before God, meaning our prayers bombard the throne of God.

But in the wilderness as the children of Israel complained, grumbling is what went up before God. So that is what God responded to. I have always been mindful of what comes out of my mouth because I want to make sure I don't speak negatively over what God considers to be a blessing.

What if the children of Israel had requested water and food instead of grumbling about it? What if they had really grasped that the God who raised up a leader, brought them out of Egypt, parted the Red Sea for them, and traveled with them in a pillar of cloud by day and a pillar of fire by night would never leave them thirsty or hungry? God is attracted to the sound of prayer, praise, and adoration. When we cry out, we build two-way communication. When we do nothing but complain and grumble, there is no conversation, no relationship.

FIGHTING SILENCE

One of the things that is so amazing to me is what happened at my college in Alabama when two or three of us gathered in our dorm room to pray. It was not a large group, but it was a group that released a sound. In chapter 2, I talked about how many times we were thrown out of the dormitory because our prayers and praise were too loud. But each time God gave us even more territory. We would leave the dorm and head out to parks and other areas on campus, often leading those in our path to Christ. Regardless of what you're walking through, don't ever allow life or a situation to silence your prayers.

The truth is the enemy thrives in silence. I believe one of the major things he wants to do is to muzzle the church because a silent church is an unprotected and vulnerable church. That's why Scripture says, "Make a joyful noise to the LORD, all the earth!" (Ps. 100:1, ESV).

I realized that the only way I could lead and protect God's people was by making prayer the number one priority in our church. So on the second and fourth Tuesday of each month, our church gathers at 4:00 a.m. to pray. After about a year or two of meeting, I sensed the Lord saying, "Make room for more." At the time, we were meeting in a building that seated about three hundred. The larger building a block away seats eleven hundred. So at four o'clock in the morning, with everyone gathered in the smaller building, I said to them, "We're now going to leave this building, and we're going to walk to the larger church. We're about to make room for more people to come to prayer." At four in the morning, one hundred and fifty people were traipsing through the streets of Chicago to make room for more people, to make room for more sound. And because we made room, more people showed up, and the sound got louder.

One of the major schemes of the enemy is to muzzle the church.

For eleven years regardless of the weather, we've come together to release the sound. Now, because of social media, anyone can join. It's open to the world. So we can average between fifteen thousand and twenty thousand people at one gathering. That prayer meeting has been integral to the life and strength of our church.

We also have multiple prayer events throughout the year. Eight years ago, I led a twenty-four-hour prayer shut-in. It almost killed me. After it was over, I said, "I'll never do this again." So now for the last six years, we've held a twelve-hour prayer event from noon to midnight in our church. First, we gathered in one of our smaller buildings, and that was good. Then we moved into the larger building, and two years ago, for the first time, we rented out a convention center—for a prayer meeting. We bring in different people who are known for their prayer lives and let them lead us in prayer. In 2020, because of the pandemic, we couldn't gather physically. But I believe so strongly in the power of prayer that I tasked our team with finding another way to hold the event. So we turned it into a prayer conference and asked people to register. Our sound won't be stopped.

We asked the speakers to set up their own environments of prayer in their different states. We had a virtual breakout session called the Mentorship Room during which each speaker talked. We offered a breakout session called the Classroom, where we taught people how to build up their prayer life. And then there was the Worship Room, which was nothing but twelve hours of worship music. God moved mightily. He exceeded my vision. Sixty-two hundred people from all over the world—New Zealand, Africa, Canada, Malaysia, Australia—convened online for prayer. So many people said they needed to be in prayer and to gather with people of like mind and heart. One woman told me, "I needed to be with others who believe what I believe and pray over everything that's happening in our world." There was no way we were going to let the pandemic stop the sound.

My assignment is clear. In Matthew 12:29, Jesus told the parable of the strong man. If a thief comes to a house, the first thing he would want to do is bind the strong man.

His thinking is, "If I bind the strong man, then I can get the house." As a pastor, I have to understand my position. I am the strong man. If the enemy wants to get into the house, he's going to hit my leadership team and me first. But if our leadership puts a demand on the house to pray, we can ask God to mightily protect the house.

Carrying the Weight

Earlier we looked at Jehoshaphat, king of Judah, and his response when he heard that three vast armies were coming for him. The moment he heard his kingdom was in danger, he immediately called for corporate prayer. He didn't go it alone. He called for the sound. He called for all of Judah to fast and pray. Second Chronicles 20:5 says Jehoshaphat stood before Israel and prayed. And in the midst of that prayer gathering—in the midst of that sound—Jahaziel stood up and delivered a prophetic word giving the Lord's solution. By turning to others to help him create the sound, Jehoshaphat had assistance carrying the weight of that imminent threat.

I can say candidly that leading God's people is very trying. One of the hardest things in the Bible for me to read is when God told Moses, "Get up. I'm going to let you look at Canaan, but you can't go in." (See Deuteronomy 34:4–5.) He couldn't go in because in the wilderness when the people were pressuring him, he didn't do what God told him to do. He did what he wanted to do. Instead of standing and letting God be glorified as the rock miraculously released water, out of anger Moses struck the rock with his staff twice, turning the spotlight on himself. (See Numbers 20:1–13.) I teach church leaders that they need a team that can discern things they might not be able to see, because sometimes in leadership, you can feel like you're out there flailing by yourself with a vast army coming after you. Sometimes as a leader, you feel as if you are the only one being hit.

Eleven years ago, I felt the need to ask our congregation to pray for God to give clarity and direction to our church. I knew I needed to hear from God, but I didn't want to carry that weight on my own. I needed to release the corporate prayer, the corporate sound, and invite everyone into this to help carry the weight. Many times, joining a symphony of interceding believers is what we need to carry on and move forward.

What's more, praying with others can release power that brings miracles! We have tons of stories of God working miracles through corporate prayer in our church. But one of my favorites is about a boy named Devin, who has grown up in our church. When Devin was born, his intestines were liquefied. Doctors told his parents, "You should prepare for your son to die." Immediately, our church went into prayer. The doctors said, "If he lives, he won't be able to hear." Devin is eleven. He can hear. He can talk. And Devin can pray. He's a miracle! He's a kid with special needs. But his wisdom, insight, and prayer life are not the norm. *He* is not the norm.

In the previous chapter, I shared about how our church has persevered in prayer as we bought buildings to make room for more people. During that process, just knowing our whole church was praying for direction gave me the stamina I needed. As I realized we were going to need to build, the City of Chicago told me, "You will not be able to build here. There's no room for you. You have no choice but to move to the suburbs." I know for a fact that I'm not called to the suburbs.

> Many times, joining a symphony of interceding believers is what we need to carry on and move forward.

Now remember, the whole church is praying together; everyone is carrying the weight, asking for direction and clarity. One day during all of this, I was driving down the street when the Lord said to me, "I need you to begin to buy every vacant lot on this side of the street, every home that is boarded up on this street." It took us three years to buy four blocks of buildings. God gave us every house, every lot. As I mentioned previously, we even purchased a factory and turned that into our children's center.

The city told us that the railroad company owned some of the land on that block. No matter what we did, the railroad company just didn't respond to us. I encouraged our church to keep praying. That's when one of our guys hopped on a plane to Atlanta and camped out at the railroad office. The man we were trying to reach walked in and said, "How did you know I was going to be here today?" Our church member didn't know, but God did. In the end, the railroad basically gave us the land.

This happened as a result of prayers being lifted throughout our church. The morning we received word that the railroad land would be ours, God gave me a word: "The earth will yield what belongs to you." These aren't things you just hear. These aren't things that just happen. You can't have these results without people raising their voices and releasing the sound. It doesn't happen on your own. I understand you may not have a whole congregation you can call on to pray with you. That's why it's so important to have a small community of believers you can go to and ask them to pray with you. Some petitions may need to remain secret that you continue to silently wrap in prayer, especially those callings and a destiny that feel bigger than us. But in the trials and confusing times of our lives, that's when it's time to call in the troops.

We not only have the prayers of others to help carry the weight of our struggles. We can also think of prayer as our greatest weapon against the enemy. Turn the page to discover how time on your knees prepares you for the battle.

LET'S TALK

- When was the last time you asked others to pray for you?
- What doors have the prayers of others opened for you?
- How have your prayers for others broken chains?
- How has other people praying for you changed your life?
- How are you praying for your pastor?
- What sound can you release to compel God to look your way?

Chapter 12

IN THE BATTLE

Do Our Prayers Really Stop the Enemy?

Take up your positions; stand firm and see the deliverance the LORD will give you, Judah and Jerusalem. Do not be afraid; do not be discouraged. Go out to face them tomorrow, and the LORD will be with you.
—2 CHRONICLES 20:17

FOR TWENTY-FOUR DAYS, he had been mourning and fasting, to the point that his skin had grown dry and weathered. For twenty-four days, he had been praying and waiting for the Lord to tell him the meaning of the vision he had seen about the destiny of his people and a great war. He had set his heart to understand, but he'd heard nothing. Finally, on the twenty-fourth day he got revelation—and it was epic! Daniel met a man whose face shined like lightning and whose eyes looked like flaming torches. Soon he learned that because of his prayers, there had been fighting in the spiritual realm. Let's read the Scripture passage. It's too good not to catch each word:

> Do not be afraid, Daniel. Since the first day that you set your mind to gain understanding and to humble yourself before your God, your words were

> heard, and I have come in response to them. But the prince of the Persian kingdom resisted me twenty-one days. Then Michael, one of the chief princes, came to help me, because I was detained there with the king of Persia. Now I have come to explain to you what will happen to your people in the future.
>
> —DANIEL 10:12–14

For three weeks, the Lord's angel and Satan's demon (Scripture calls the spiritual adversary the prince of Persia) warred with each other. Finally, the angel of God prevailed and arrived to unpack everything Daniel had seen in the vision. The account is a vivid, detailed picture of what goes on in the spiritual realm when we pray. The Book of Daniel reveals to us that just as the spiritual realm impacts what happens here on earth, our prayers carry weight in the spiritual realm.

Don't miss that. There is a constant battle raging, and our prayers are part of it. In Ephesians 6:12, the apostle Paul tells us that "our struggle is not against flesh and blood, but against the rulers, against the authorities, against the powers of this dark world and against the spiritual forces of evil in the heavenly realms." And in the same chapter, he goes on to talk about the armor of God. He knows there is a spiritual battle taking place in the unseen.

Satan tries to block the answer to your prayers; he attempts to detain you—he'll do anything and everything he can do to wedge himself between you and God. That's why God gave us prayer. Our prayers—our relationship with our Creator and Savior—are our greatest weapon in the battle. The truth is that believing and trusting God is warfare. Maintaining your faith is warfare. Monitoring yourself while you wait is warfare. Keeping negative people out of your spirit is warfare. And we fight all these battles on our knees. When you pray, you're fighting against the spiritual forces of evil. You're participating in spiritual warfare that's happening around you each day and every moment. There's so much more happening than what we see in the natural world.

> Our prayers—our relationship with our Creator and Savior—are our greatest weapon in the battle.

Really, everything we've been talking about in this book so far—understanding why we've been called to pray, learning how to pray, persevering in our prayers, and calling on others to gather and pray with us—leads up to this, because a rich prayer life arms us to fight the enemy that prowls, kills, and seeks to destroy (John 10:10; 1 Pet. 5:8). It cultivates unshakable faith that withstands our enemy no matter how long and how hard he fights to detain us. See why I've been telling you to just pray? There's so much power in those two small words.

Take Up Your Position

In preparation to write this chapter, I interviewed a US Army commander I know. I wanted to hear firsthand about military strategy on the battlefield. He told me that every military strategist knows that position is key to winning any battle: "A victory starts with maneuvering your troops to the most advantageous position and then taking your position on the battlefield to defend your territory and take your enemy's territory."[1] He pointed me to a book called *The Art of War*, written by an ancient Chinese general named Sun Tzu, who was known as a brilliant military strategist. His book is considered to be one of the world's most influential works on military strategy. I confess I didn't read the book; however, I did stumble onto a website with one hundred quotes from the book. Two thousand years ago Sun Tzu said the same thing my army friend said two weeks ago. So much of his strategy relied on the importance of taking up your position. One of his quotes stuck with me: "You can be sure of succeeding in your attacks if you only attack places which are undefended."[2]

On our knees in prayer, we go on the defensive and offensive—asking God to defend our hearts and embolden us to take territory for Him. I think of David after the massacre at Ziklag in 1 Samuel 30. While David and his men were away, the Amalekites raided the city and burned it, taking captive everyone in it, including David's two wives. When David and his men returned to Ziklag and saw what had been done, Scripture says they wept out loud until they had no strength left to weep. And the men became so bitter that they started talking about stoning David. That's when David took up the position and got down on his knees in prayer. As he prayed, he was encouraged. Verse 6 says, "But David found strength in the LORD his God." God bolstered him to the point that David went on the offensive and asked God, "Lord, shall I pursue?" God told him, "Pursue and you will recover all." Basically, "Get off the defense and let's go on the offense and get your stuff."

We've talked a lot about the Judean King Jehoshaphat and how he took his position on his knees (and called his kingdom to do the same) when he heard that his enemies were coming for Judah. But I want you to notice what happens as this story progresses. In 2 Chronicles 20:17, God tells Jehoshaphat, "You will not have to fight the battle." From there, He continues (and this is what I really want you to get): "Take up your positions; stand firm and see the deliverance the LORD will give you....Do not be afraid; do not be discouraged. Go out to face them tomorrow, and the LORD will be with you."

Did you catch that? "Take up your positions" and "stand firm"—that's doing battle. "Do not be afraid; do not be discouraged"—that's doing battle. "Go out and face them tomorrow"—that's engaging in warfare. And as you take up this position, the Lord will be with you. Look at what Jehoshaphat does in verse 18: "Jehoshaphat bowed down with his face to the ground, and all the people of Judah and Jerusalem fell down in worship before the LORD." That's the position! We can either take up the position of humility and let the Lord fight for us, or we can choose to fight in our own strength (by the way, that's called pride). This passage is so important for us today. Too many of us are fighting our own battles. I don't know about you, but the times I've tried to fight in my own strength haven't worked out too well.

Sometimes taking up the position looks like intercession. Chicago is a very violent city. For the last eight or nine years, every June our church has organized a citywide prayer line down a street in the city known for gang activity. About three thousand people line up for a solid two miles to pray together for our city and its youth. We seek the Lord's face together, and collectively, we pray against the enemy's schemes. We place a prayer leader on every corner with a bullhorn. One year, we asked parents who have lost kids to violence to bring a picture of their children and hold it. We wanted to make sure they're not forgotten. Through our intercession, we're fighting what I believe is a very spiritual battle. Since we've been praying like this, the city has seen violence on this street decrease. Praise God!

Your specific petition on the battlefield won't always be the same. Some days you'll be praying for more territory. Other days you'll be praying for protection. Sometimes you'll be interceding for others or your city and country. But whatever the battle looks like, your position is the same: on your knees "just praying."

Stay Your Position

In Exodus 17, the Amalekites were threatening the Israelites. Moses told Joshua to choose some men to fight. Then Moses revealed his war strategy: during the battle he would stand on the top of the hill overlooking the battlefield with the staff of God in his hands. The next day, Moses climbed to the top of the hill and raised the staff. As long as his arms were up, Israel prevailed. But as soon as he let down his arm, the battle shifted, and the Amalekites gained ground. Thankfully, Moses had the forethought to bring backup. Aaron and Hur flanked him, so when Moses' arms grew tired, Aaron and Hur were there to steady and support them, and Israel emerged victorious.

That night, Moses built an altar and called it "The Lord is my Banner" (Exod. 17:15). Moses got it. He understood that the battle is the Lord's. Moses did what military strategists call "staying your position." And God used Moses to show the children of Israel *His* power. That's why I've always loved this story. How can you not? It's such a picture of God's faithfulness to fight our battles when we get on our knees and stand firm.

> Whatever the battle looks like, your position is the same: on your knees "just praying."

Moses and Jehoshaphat show us that taking up your position and maintaining your position go hand in hand. If we go back to Daniel 10, Scripture tells us that Daniel had been praying and fasting for three weeks, desperately waiting for an answer from God. He did not shift; he did not move. He stayed his position. He was where he was supposed to be to receive the answer—still speaking to God, still waiting on Him as the battle raged in the spiritual realm. I can imagine those three weeks were some of Daniel's darkest hours (and if you know his story, this man of God had a lot of dark hours in exile). Unknowingly he was involved in a war raging in the heavens. Staying his position until he received spiritual understanding of the vision meant life or death for his people.

The same battles are happening today. Satan tries to detain us. He attempts to move us, to shift us. He wants nothing more than to see us distracted, bitter, prideful—off our knees, defenseless, and vulnerable to his attack. As we've followed God's leading and vision for this new church campus, I've learned a lot about not only taking up my position but also maintaining it. As believers, we want the favor of God. We want the Lord's blessings. All of it comes with a test, with people having an opinion, with people saying anything and attempting to do anything to shift or knock you from your position of prayer. If you're not careful, you'll become reactive. You'll react to every lie. You'll react to every criticism and everything you uncover.

I have had to deal with the challenges that come with being used by God on an elevated platform—people throwing stones and plotting attacks. As we began to build our church, people criticized me, saying, "We don't need another church in the Black community." Others criticized me because the church wasn't built as fast as I thought it would be. The news media came out and questioned me, reporting on "the church they have been building for five years." It hasn't really been five years, but the media put it out there. Social media is horrible because anybody and everybody can attack you on social media. People posted all sorts of cruel things like, "He's building a church that's not ever going to be built."

> Satan tries to detain us. He attempts to move us, to shift us. He wants nothing more than to see us distracted, bitter, prideful—off our knees, defenseless, and vulnerable to his attack.

The battle raged on. Someone who used to work at our church lied and said that our COO stole two million dollars from me. That's when the contractor quit the whole job. This is a union city. I decided to hire a non-union contractor because a union one would have cost three million dollars more. That was money I didn't have. So the union picketed and tried to block the work trucks. They even blew up a big rat in front of our building with a message that I am "a rat in the city" because I didn't hire union. Every time the construction company told me the building was going to be ready, it wasn't. Not to mention the fact that people whom you're building for are no longer with you for whatever reason. That's enough to break the average person. I believe it would have broken me if I had not stayed my position in prayer. I knew I hadn't heard wrong even when some people in the community and city tried to tell me I had. I continued to "call to mind" (remember chapter 6, on thankfulness) what God had done: "God, You gave us all this land. You literally let us buy four blocks of land in a big city. You have done too much for me to get here for me to think You're going to abandon me."

In so many ways, God protected our church completely unbeknownst to us. I shared this earlier, but it's a good reminder. When COVID-19 showed up, the city shut down. All the construction froze. Had construction been completed, we would have been left paying a mortgage on a building no one would be able to use for months. You have to maintain your position and stand firm because you *will* see the salvation of the Lord. You *will* see Him fight the battle for you.

In the Waiting

This may be the most difficult and dangerous area of spiritual warfare: the waiting period that happens pre-battle as well as during the fight before the victor is revealed. In the waiting, we have to monitor our words and what we're putting into our minds and hearts. We have to do everything possible to make sure we stay focused. And we do that through prayer.

One of the greatest professions in the middle of battle is what David said to Goliath: "This day the Lord will give you into my hands.…All those gathered here will know that it is not by sword or spear that the Lord saves; for the battle is the Lord's" (1 Sam. 17:46–47). Don't miss this—David killed Goliath with his words before he killed him with the stone. We tend to focus on the one smooth stone it took to kill Goliath. I wish more Sunday schools would back up and teach what I believe is the most critical part of this story.

Think about everything that was against David: size, strength, even those around him. Only days before, King Saul had told David, "You are not able to go out against this Philistine and fight him; you are only a young man, and he has been a warrior from his youth" (1 Sam. 17:33). On the day of the battle, Goliath said almost the same thing as he taunted his opponent. When David stepped onto the battlefield, the giant warrior was indignant: "Am I a dog, that you come at me with sticks?" (1 Sam. 17:43).

I wonder how much had gone into the waiting period between when Samuel anointed David to be king and that day. We don't know the secret petitions of David's heart. Is it possible that David had been praying his whole life while he was tending the flocks? It's possible that David immediately began to pray when Goliath stepped onto the battlefield, but something tells me he had been talking to God all his life. Otherwise, he wouldn't have been ready to stand firm, slay the giant with his words (the first weapon he used), and then seal the deal with the stone. In the waiting, David took his position, and in the throes of battle, he stayed firm.

Recently I watched the movie *Thirteen Days*, about the Cuban missile crisis and everything that happened in the thirteen days before the United States reached an agreement with the Soviet Union to prevent nuclear war. Throughout the movie several US leaders were called upon to communicate the US position. At one point the US ambassador to the United Nations, Adlai Stevenson, had to blatantly confront the Soviet ambassador about the missiles the United States sighted in Cuba. He was charged with convincing the UN representatives that the US position was prudent and important. The United States desperately needed him to take his position and not back down, to stand firm and secure political buy-in for a blockade of Cuba. His political victory in the waiting period was critical to the outcome of that crisis, which (so far) is the closest the world has ever come to nuclear war.

The waiting period and what we do in it are a critical part of the battle with our enemy. Resisting the temptation to take matters into our own hands, try to figure it out, put our hands on it, run to a temporary and man-made solution—that's part of the battle, and the only thing that will keep your flesh under subjection is prayer. How you respond in the waiting is critical.

Reposition and Refocus

When we were in the throes of building our campus, I went to Australia to preach at a conference, and when I went to comb my hair, all my hair came out in big clumps. Back at home, I went to the barber, and he was like, "*Whoa!*" One of my friends suggested I see a doctor. I pulled out a picture of my hair from a month before, and the doctor immediately knew something wasn't right. It was stress. My hair was literally falling out because of the stress I was under. That was how my body was reacting. Thank God only my hair was affected. Stress can lead to heart attack, stroke, and any number of potentially fatal or debilitating conditions.

> The waiting period and what we do in it are a critical part of the battle with our enemy.

Nevertheless, it was a wake-up call. I knew I had to reposition myself and not let everything that was happening weigh on me like it was. I knew I couldn't take on the stress of looking at everything I was facing, the stress of reading what everybody was posting, the stress of who was leaving the church—it was all way, way, way too much. I had to open my eyes and see the salvation of the Lord. For me, repositioning and refocusing meant making intentional choices. I kept looking at everything God was doing and continued to profess to our church, "The world is in a recession, but we're not participating." And during the building process, I avoided looking at the construction site. Even on Sundays, I couldn't drive by it, because I knew I wasn't in a place to see it. Weeks went by, and I didn't see the building.

In the throes of the pandemic, I went on the offensive and defensive. I prayed live online every Tuesday and every Friday at 7:00 p.m. I watched the news only so I could discern what to pray about when we gathered live. During the peak of the racial tensions in 2020, there were some things I chose not to watch. Part of spiritual warfare is asking God to guard your heart. This is the time when you admit when you're not strong—when you admit you're vulnerable, that you're too open. God has filled His Book with warnings and admonitions to protect your heart:

Keep your heart with all vigilance, for from it flow the springs of life.

—Proverbs 4:23

Do not be anxious about anything, but in everything by prayer and supplication with thanksgiving let your requests be made known to God. And the peace of God, which surpasses all understanding, will guard your hearts and your minds in Christ Jesus.

—Philippians 4:6–7

Finally, brothers and sisters, whatever is true, whatever is noble, whatever is right, whatever is pure, whatever is lovely, whatever is admirable—if anything is excellent or praiseworthy—think about such things.

—Philippians 4:8

Create in me a clean heart, O God, and renew a right spirit within me.

—Psalm 51:10

Do not be conformed to this world, but be transformed by the renewal of your mind, that by testing you may discern what is the will of God, what is good and acceptable and perfect.

—Romans 12:2

Do not give dogs what is holy, and do not throw your pearls before pigs, lest they trample them underfoot and turn to attack you.

—Matthew 7:6

I know one of the things that has saved me during all of this is the consistency of our 4:00 a.m. prayer we've been holding for more than a decade. That saves me because it makes me crawl right back into my spot: on my hands and knees. It keeps me broken. It keeps me at His feet. It keeps me reminding Him that this battle is not mine; it's His. You will get to a point where you do not have what it takes, where if God doesn't do it, it won't get done. I'll tell you firsthand, when you reach that place, it's difficult to keep going. I had to understand and truly trust that delay doesn't mean deny. Let me say that again: *Delay doesn't mean deny.*

> Part of spiritual warfare is asking God to guard your heart. This is the time when you admit when you're not strong.

We have to reposition ourselves—going back down to our faces, each time remembering our salvation and how far God has brought us. He has given us instructions for living in this world today. Following those instructions is the warfare. It's why the apostle Paul says, "I beat my body under subjection; I make it do what it needs to do." (See 1 Corinthians 9:27.) The whole time the spiritual battle is raging. The detractors don't stop. But with prayer, we can reposition and refocus—all the while building up an unshakable faith.

THE BATTLE IS HIS

Recently, I heard a story from a believer in India that brought me to my knees in praise. He told me how his family was praying and worshipping in their home (they were the only Christians in their village but had started a small house church) when a village mob surrounded their house. In parts of India, especially remote areas, Christians who have left Hinduism or the tribal religion are excommunicated, often deprived of water and food sources. Sometimes they're physically attacked for following Jesus. In more than sixty countries, the persecution we read about in the Bible is still happening today.

Delay doesn't mean deny.

This Christian continued his story: "As the mob called for us to come out, we prayed that God would be with us. We stepped out, and as we walked toward them, we saw terror in their faces. They were pointing at the sky as they backed away from us. We looked behind us, and in the sky we saw multitudes of armies. It had to be the Lord's armies protecting us."

I understand that story may be hard to believe, especially if you live in the Western world. We don't tend to see this kind of concrete evidence. Yet in places like India, Africa, and the Middle East, Christians speak of divine visions and dreams often. But seen or unseen, I can tell you that there are spiritual battles happening around us every day—in our hearts, our minds, our desires, our families, our workplaces, our words, our actions. My guess is you're feeling that. You get that what's at work in our world today is much greater and much darker than human or earthly actions.

As Christians, we know Jesus has already defeated Satan (Col. 2:15), but that doesn't mean Satan won't do everything in his power to make you lose sight of that. He intends to keep you discouraged and defeated. More than that, Scripture tells us he's like a lion that shrewdly and determinedly prowls, seeking to kill and destroy its prey. Our enemy is hell-bent on taking our lives. Don't ever think he's out for anything less. One of the military tactics Sun Tzu highlights in *The Art of War* speaks to that: "He who exercises no forethought but makes light of his opponents is sure to be captured by them."[3] It's a sobering truth.

> What's at work in our world today is much greater and much darker than human or earthly actions.

But just like in the story this Indian believer shared, we're not alone in this war. Far from it. The battle is the Lord's. The prophecy Jehoshaphat was given, the revelation Daniel received, and the declaration David shouted—they all show us that God is our warrior. We have divine soldiers fighting for us. Even when the world is shaking, I know that God's got this! He's got you! I love what happens after the Lord's messenger told Daniel what happened in the spiritual realm. The man with the flaming eyes is ready to move forward and reveal the meaning of Daniel's end times vision, but the Hebrew has no strength left. Scripture says his face turned deathly pale, and he was helpless. Read Daniel's account of what happened next:

> A hand touched me and set me trembling on my hands and knees. He said, "Daniel, you who are highly esteemed, consider carefully the words I am about to speak to you, and stand up, for I have now been sent to you." And when he said this to me, I stood up trembling....
>
> While he was saying this to me, I bowed with my

> face toward the ground and was speechless. Then one who looked like a man touched my lips, and I opened my mouth and began to speak. I said to the one standing before me, "I am overcome with anguish because of the vision, my LORD, and I feel very weak. How can I, your servant, talk with you, my LORD? My strength is gone and I can hardly breathe." Again the one who looked like a man touched me and gave me strength. "Do not be afraid, you who are highly esteemed," he said. "Peace! Be strong now; be strong."
>
> When he spoke to me, I was strengthened and said, "Speak, my LORD, since you have given me strength." So he said, "Do you know why I have come to you? Soon I will return to fight against the prince of Persia, and when I go, the prince of Greece will come; but first I will tell you what is written in the Book of Truth."
>
> —DANIEL 4:10–11, 15–21

My friend, you already have what Daniel received. Do you get that? You have the Holy Spirit fighting for you and angels touching you when you're weak and encouraging you to stand when you can take no more. You have Christ who heals you when you're wounded and can't see what He's doing. You have a God who imparts to you the peace that transcends all human understanding and gives you His strength to move you forward into battle and onto the battlefield.

All of this is yours when you just pray.

LET'S TALK

- How has your approach to spiritual warfare transformed or evolved since you began reading this book?
- Do you believe that what we're seeing in our world today is a spiritual battle? Why or why not?
- Did you ever think prayer could be so critical to spiritual warfare before reading this chapter? Why or why not?
- What can you start doing today to prepare yourself and be ready for the battle?

CONCLUSION

His people—young and old; men, women, and children—would be destroyed on a single day. When Mordecai learned about Haman's wicked plan to annihilate the Jewish people, he tore his clothes, put on the customary sackcloth, and went out into the city, wailing loudly. And now we have one of the most powerful back-and-forths in history. Mordecai went to the king's gate and sent a message to Queen Esther, his niece and adoptive daughter, telling her about the planned genocide. Esther's reply must have been so discouraging. She wrote:

> All the king's officials and the people of the royal provinces know that for any man or woman who approaches the king in the inner court without being summoned the king has but one law: that they be put to death unless the king extends the gold scepter to them and spares their lives. But thirty days have passed since I was called to go to the king.
>
> —Esther 4:11

Still, Mordecai didn't give up. He pressed on, sending another message to Esther, telling her that she and her father's family would not be spared just because she was in the king's house. And this is what I want you to get. Mordecai said:

> For if you remain silent at this time, relief and deliverance for the Jews will arise from another place,

> but you and your father's family will perish. And who knows but that you have come to your royal position for such a time as this?
>
> —ESTHER 4:14

For such a time as this. With those words, Esther resolved to speak to King Xerxes—even if it meant her death. In desperation and with boldness, she interceded for her people. Esther recognized that she had been placed in the palace for a purpose.

Friend, I hope you realize that everything we've talked about in these last twelve chapters is for such a time as this. When I started thinking about this book, there was no way of knowing everything that would happen in 2020. None of us knew the desperate times we would be in not only in America but throughout the world. It's as if the levees have broken. Few of us will forget when New Orleans' levees broke in 2005 and the massive destruction Hurricane Katrina caused as a result.

The earth is groaning. I can feel it and hear it. I'm sure you can too.

During our church's June prayer gathering, sixty-two hundred people gathered to pray and hear testimonies. Because of the pandemic, we were forced to host the event online, which turned out to be a huge blessing. Our live-turned-virtual event grew into a global conference with people from Ghana, Kenya, the United Kingdom, and more tuning in. The whole time, I heard and read comments from participants around the globe about how they really needed that time to pray together with like-minded people. Many said it brought spiritual balm to their souls.

Since the onset of the pandemic, I've been asked to pray

for an organization in Ghana. I've prayed for a church in Nigeria. I've been called into prayer meetings from around the world. Make no mistake. The whole world has been praying, asking God for healing.

The earth is groaning. I can feel it and hear it. I'm sure you can too.

All of us—Christian or not—are searching for something to grab on to, something that's not going to shift when everything else is moving and even shaking. The question is, What will you grasp? Will it be the unconditional love of Christ or will it be your 401(k), your spouse, your church, your pastor, your career, your fill-in-the-blank?

Peace and Deliverance Start With Prayer

As God's people, we need to be down on our knees, interceding for our world and for those around us. Bottom line: Our world needs peace, and we won't get there without prayer. Peace starts with talking to our Creator and Savior.

I think of Paul and Silas in a jail cell, their feet fastened in stocks. They had already been severely flogged. Yet Scripture says they were singing and worshipping to the point that others heard it. Their prayers and petitions raised to heaven caused the earth to shake. *Boom*! The prison door was opened, and the chains were broken. (See Acts 16:16–40.) The miracle God worked that night started with Peter's and Silas' perseverance to pray and their unshakable faith, which ensured they didn't get caught up in the difficulty and what seemed like a doomsday situation.

We must commit to fervently pray that God would open doors and break chains in our towns, our cities, our country, and the world. That's the seat of the intercessor right now. In 2 Chronicles 7:14, God tells us, "If my people, who are called by my name, will humble themselves and pray and seek my face and turn from their wicked ways, then I will hear from heaven, and I will forgive their sin and will heal their land." I'm crying out to God. I'm crying out for healing and deliverance. I'm crying out for peace.

Our world needs peace, and we won't get there without prayer.

And I know that God hears us when we pray. His Word gives us that promise: "Surely the arm of the LORD is not too short to save, nor his ear too dull to hear" (Isa. 59:1).

As an intercessor for our world, you will feel the weight—not just of your city or country; you will also feel the weight of the world. It's one of the five marks of an intercessor we talked about in chapter 8. That intercessor seat is often uncomfortable. Praying for our world often reveals our heart and deeply rooted biases or views we may not have known were even there.

Practically, interceding for our world means that you make it a priority even when something may not impact you directly. You put it on your prayer list and regularly bring it to God, making your requests known to Him. I believe God is putting this global call to pray in the hearts and spirits of praying people. We're literally crying out for the world.

Global warming may not be affecting your city, but it's affecting the world. Civil unrest may not be publicly playing out in your town, but the world is experiencing it. One of the things that blew my mind was to see the global impact of George Floyd's killing. His brutal death in Minnesota by police ignited protests as far as the UK and Africa. His photo and even the video of his killing made it to numerous countries. Yes, there's global unrest.

And I'm not shy about naming the sins. We know that God is love. Yet what we're experiencing in our world today doesn't appear to be love. There's so much bitterness, so much hatred, so much anger right now. We need all of us on our knees, countering this current state and praying for God's love, peace, and healing.

> I believe God is putting this global call to pray in the hearts and spirits of praying people.

One of the amazing things we see in the Book of Judges is that whenever the children of Israel went through a tough season and cried out to God, He would raise up a deliverer. They would win over their enemies, enjoying a season of silence—a time of no wars when everyone was able to just breathe, when there was no foolishness. Today, the earth desperately needs a season of silence.

We need Christ followers with robust prayer lives to humble themselves and pray for God's will to be done. Do you remember how America was knocked to its knees on September 11? We were humbled beyond measure. Throughout the country, churches filled with people praying, confessing and crying out to God. So we know what humility looks like. We know what it sounds like. Twenty years later, we need to be praying for the same humble attitude we saw in 2001.

Silence Is Approval

To quote a popular paraphrase of a sermon by Dr. Martin Luther King, "There comes a time when silence is betrayal....Our lives begin to end the day we become silent about things that matter....In the end, we will remember not the words of our enemies, but the silence of our friends."[1] I believe Dr. King's words wholeheartedly. He was spot-on! Our silence is betrayal. It's also approval.

But I'm here to tell you that everyone, and that includes you, needs to know their own lane or, to put it another way, where, when, and how they'll raise their voice. A movement does not include everybody doing the same thing. Just because I wasn't on the front line in the summer of 2020 marching in protests doesn't mean I wasn't doing my part. Far from it. I'm leading my church of nineteen thousand people to humble themselves and pray. You need to recognize and profess where you stand.

Exodus 32 tells us that when Moses came down from the mountain with the Ten Commandments and saw the Israelites worshipping the golden calf, he stood at the entrance to the camp and told them, "Whoever is for the Lord, come to me" (v. 26). Essentially Moses said, "Make a stand. Which side are you on?" Now hear me on this because I'm not playing around: If you're not interceding for our world in prayer, your silence indicates your approval of what's happening. Without prayer, we will stay stuck in racism and the polarization that has shaken our world. Whether the issue is within your village, your tight circle, or your family—you need to break the silence and pray.

Intercession doesn't have to be done on a large platform. *No one has to be around when you slay the giant.* The left-handed judge Ehud we read about in Judges 3 shows us that. (Be honest, did you even know there was a left-handed judge named Ehud in the Bible?) Ehud was part of the tribe of Benjamin and the one God sent to deliver the Israelites from eighteen years of Moabite domination. When Ehud went to kill the Moabite King Eglon, he closed the door behind him and privately slayed him. Some things are privately slain but publicly celebrated. Let's read the story.

> Ehud then approached him while he was sitting alone in the upper room of his palace and said, "I have a message from God for you." As the king rose from his seat, Ehud reached with his left hand, drew the sword from his right thigh and plunged it into the king's belly....After he had gone, the servants came and found the doors of the upper room locked. They said, "He must be relieving himself in the inner room of the palace."
>
> They waited to the point of embarrassment, but when he did not open the doors of the room, they took a key and unlocked them. There they saw their lord fallen to the floor, dead. While they waited, Ehud got away. He passed by the stone images and escaped to Seirah. When he arrived there, he blew a trumpet in the hill country of Ephraim, and the Israelites went down with him from the hills, with him leading them.
>
> "Follow me," he ordered, "for the LORD has given Moab, your enemy, into your hands." So they followed him down and took possession of the fords of the Jordan that led to Moab; they allowed no one to cross over. At that time they struck down about

> ten thousand Moabites, all vigorous and strong; not one escaped.
>
> —JUDGES 3:20–21, 24–29

After Ehud kills the king and the Israelites battle the Moabites, Israel has a season of silence for eighty years. Privately slaying our enemy happens in prayer, alone or with a small group of people praying with you.

THREE PRAYERS FOR PEACE

I love Moses and the story of God leading His people in Exodus. You probably realize that by now. Let's back up about ten chapters from where we were in the last section and look at everything that happened to bring the Israelites out of Egypt. In Exodus 14, the Israelites are at the Red Sea. Now remember everything they've recently witnessed: the ten plagues, the Passover, deliverance, their release and even the wealth they took from Egypt. But here they are, with Pharaoh's army in sight on one side and the Red Sea on the other side. And the Bible says they were "terrified." See what they said to Moses: "Was it because there were no graves in Egypt that you brought us to the desert to die? What have you done to us by bringing us out of Egypt? Didn't we say to you in Egypt, 'Leave us alone; let us serve the Egyptians'? It would have been better for us to serve the Egyptians than to die in the desert!" (Exod. 14:11–12).

> Whether the issue is within your village, your tight circle, or your family—you need to break the silence and pray.

Do you see what happened? Their fear made them forget every miracle they had seen God work in their lives.

Listen to me: Fear will make you draw a blank. And fear will keep you from seeing victory. This I recall; therefore I have hope. Moses says, "Do not be afraid, you will never see these Egyptians again. Don't lose your faith." (See Exodus 14:13.) Fear will stop you from seeing victory. Fear will stop you from moving. It's paralyzing. The Israelites were unable to move, unable to recall in their minds and hearts everything they had seen God do. So here at the end of our time together, it seems fitting that I leave you with prayers to help you combat fear. I'm not playing around. I'm sick of the devil, and I'm sick of the torment. I want to give you three prayers for peace—peace in our world, peace in your surroundings, and peace in your mind.

A Prayer for Peace in Our World

> *God, I pray for peace on this earth. I pray against the spirit of division, of injustice, of conflict, and of confrontation. So many are on edge today. I come against a lack of faith in You and ask that peace be on this earth right now. In every country, every village, in the backwoods, in the concrete jungles, I ask You to breathe on us and let there be peace. I bind the spirit of fear that has paralyzed people. I intercede for our various cities. I ask for peace in our community, our city, our state, our country, and the world. I come against racial profiling and fear of police. I come against prejudice and racism. I rebuke the agitators who stir up aggravation and want to ignite fires. I come against the words of hatred that have been released. I come against police*

brutality and those who are attacking police. I come against the spirit of violence. O God, would You release peace on this earth?

A Prayer for Peace in Your Environment/Surroundings

God, I pray that our homes be places of peace. I ask You to cover our houses, our neighborhood blocks, our community. I pray, God, that there would be peace in our families, our jobs, and in our churches. I pray over marriages and single parents. I come against the enemy that wants to disturb our peace. I come against conflicts with in-laws. I pray for peace on our jobs, on our commutes. I pray against road rage. God, when I walk into a room, I want to represent peace. I want peace coming out of my pores. Would You help me radiate peace? Would You help me to control my tongue? I pray that our kids will have peace when they go out of the house. I pray for peace in our schools. Father, protect our students and teachers. If I am housing any anger, I pray that You would show me my heart. I come against physical abuse, emotional abuse, spiritual abuse. This battle is not mine; it is Yours. I pray for the wisdom and self-control to hold my tongue and control my attitude. O God, You are the Prince of Peace over our environment.

A Prayer for Peace Over Your Mind

God, I pray that You would give me the mind of Christ. Would You watch over my thought pattern? I pray that You would give me the ability to decree that whatever things are lovely, whatever things are noble, whatever things are beautiful, whatever things are pure—that I would begin to think on these things. I come against the spirit of offense. God, would You give me the ability to shake off any offense like Paul shook off the snake? It was there to poison him, and those around him expected Paul to die. God, I pray that those who are expecting me to break and lose it would instead see my family and me walk in victory. He whom the Son has set free is free indeed. I ask You to help me take on my new identity. To help me remember that You have started a good work in me and You will finish what You started. I pray that Your Holy Spirit would train me to always remember what You have already done. Father, remind me of who You are when I begin to feel terrified. Father, I desire to focus on what You've done in my life—not the storm that's raging. Will You help me do that? Thank You, Father, for being with me. Thank You for never leaving me.

✦

I can't tell you how much I believe this: Prayer is the strongest power on earth. Hands down. I hope you get that by now. I hope you realize this incredible weapon you have in these difficult times. You've now learned why God wants you to pray, how He wants you to pray, and how we develop a life of prayer that leads to unshakable faith. You have words of adoration, scriptures of thankfulness, and specific prayers at your fingertips.

Now the questions are: What are you going to do with all of it? How are you going to use it to bring you closer to Christ and intercede for others? How will you find ways to gather with others and build your prayer village? How will you teach others to pray and cultivate a desire to pray more? Will you commit to praying fervently for your family, your community, your county, your region, your state, your country, and your world?

I'm praying for you as you answer and walk out these questions. I love you. I believe your prayers will change our world. And I'm honored to pray alongside you. I even ask you to pray for me. By now, you know me pretty well. Please pray for me as I lead others to seek God's face in prayer. I don't think it's a happy coincidence you have this book in your hands (or on your screen) and that you're here with me at the end. God has providentially brought us together.

I believe your prayers will change our world.

Believe me when I say that so much can happen in your life, in the lives of those around you, and in our world when you focus on those two small words: "just pray." It seems only fitting that I close our time together with a scripture—Jesus' words to His disciples (then and now). I earnestly pray that you'll cling to His promise today and in the years ahead as you cultivate a life of prayer that builds unwavering, undaunted, unshakable faith.

> I've told you all this so that trusting me, you will be *unshakable* and assured, deeply at *peace*. In this godless world you will continue to experience difficulties. But take heart! I've conquered the world.
>
> —John 16:33, MSG, emphasis added

Appendix A

WORDS OF ADORATION

I'VE BEEN USING this list—and adding to it—for years, and it continues to bless me. I've included it here to serve as a tool to help you express your adoration to God. Say, "Lord, You are…" before each word or phrase, and focus on Him and how worthy He is.

all I have
all I need
all I want
all-powerful
all wise
amazing
Emmanuel
glorious
good
great
Jehovah Jireh
Jehovah Rapha
like no other
magnificent
mighty
my all in all
my Abba Father
my defender
my Champion
my closest friend
my cornerstone
my Counselor
my Deliverer
my Father
my foundation
my healer
my hero
my hiding place

my high tower

my joy

my Messiah

my peace

my portion

my protector

my Redeemer

my refuge

my respite

my rock

my superman

my waymaker

sovereign in all Your ways

strong

the air I breathe

the alert God

the aware God

the beat of my heart

the center of my joy

the God who never slumbers

the God who reigns

the lover of my soul

the Prince of Peace

the skip in my step

the smile on my face

wonderful

Appendix B

SCRIPTURES EXPRESSING THANKFULNESS

Adapt the following scriptures into prayers to express your gratitude for who God is and all He has done.

With praise and thanksgiving they sang to the Lord: "He is good; his love toward Israel endures forever." And all the people gave a great shout of praise to the Lord, because the foundation of the house of the Lord was laid.

—Ezra 3:11

I will give thanks to the Lord because of his righteousness; I will sing the praises of the name of the Lord Most High.

—Psalm 7:17

I will give thanks to you, Lord, with all my heart; I will tell of all your wonderful deeds.

—Psalm 9:1

I will give you thanks in the great assembly; among the throngs I will praise you.

—Psalm 35:18

I will praise God's name in song and glorify him with thanksgiving.

—PSALM 69:30

Come, let us sing for joy to the LORD; let us shout aloud to the Rock of our salvation. Let us come before him with thanksgiving and extol him with music and song. For the LORD is the great God, the great King above all gods.

—PSALM 95:1–3

Enter his gates with thanksgiving and his courts with praise; give thanks to him and praise his name. For the LORD is good and his love endures forever; his faithfulness continues through all generations.

—PSALM 100:4–5

Praise the LORD. Give thanks to the LORD, for he is good; his love endures forever.

—PSALM 106:1

Let them give thanks to the LORD for his unfailing love and his wonderful deeds for mankind. Let them sacrifice thank offerings and tell of his works with songs of joy.

—PSALM 107:21–22

Give thanks to the LORD, for he is good; his love endures forever.

—PSALM 118:1

I thank and praise you, God of my ancestors: You have given me wisdom and power, you have made known to me what we asked of you, you have made known to us the dream of the king.

—Daniel 2:23

Be filled with the Spirit, speaking to one another with psalms, hymns, and songs from the Spirit. Sing and make music from your heart to the Lord, always giving thanks to God the Father for everything, in the name of our Lord Jesus Christ.

—Ephesians 5:18–20

Do not be anxious about anything, but in every situation, by prayer and petition, with thanksgiving, present your requests to God. And the peace of God, which transcends all understanding, will guard your hearts and your minds in Christ Jesus.

—Philippians 4:6–7

So then, just as you received Christ Jesus as Lord, continue to live your lives in him, rooted and built up in him, strengthened in the faith as you were taught, and overflowing with thankfulness.

—Colossians 2:6–7

Let the peace of Christ rule in your hearts, since as members of one body you were called to peace. And be thankful. Let the message of Christ dwell among you richly as you teach and admonish one another with all wisdom through psalms, hymns, and songs from the Spirit, singing to God with gratitude in your hearts. And whatever you do, whether in word or deed, do it all in the name of the Lord Jesus, giving thanks to God the Father through him.

—Colossians 3:15–17

Devote yourselves to prayer, being watchful and thankful.

—Colossians 4:2

Rejoice always, pray continually, give thanks in all circumstances; for this is God's will for you in Christ Jesus.

—1 Thessalonians 5:16–18

Therefore, since we are receiving a kingdom that cannot be shaken, let us be thankful, and so worship God acceptably with reverence and awe, for our "God is a consuming fire."

—Hebrews 12:28–29

Through Jesus, therefore, let us continually offer to God a sacrifice of praise—the fruit of lips that openly profess his name. And do not forget to do good and to share with others, for with such sacrifices God is pleased.

—Hebrews 13:15–16

Consider it pure joy, my brothers and sisters, whenever you face trials of many kinds, because you know that the testing of your faith produces perseverance. Let perseverance finish its work so that you may be mature and complete, not lacking anything.

—James 1:2–5

NOTES

Introduction

1. New Christian Bible Study staff, "He Shall Be as a Tree Planted by the Water," New Christian Bible Study, accessed December 8, 2020, https://newchristianbiblestudy.org/bible/story/he-shall-be-as-a-tree-planted-by-the-water/king-james-version.

Chapter 2

1. George Bush, *Notes, Critical and Practical, on the Books of Joshua and Judges: Designed as a General Help to Biblical Reading and Instruction* (New York: E. French, 1838), 295.
2. Flint Wild, "What Is a Spacewalk?" NASA, July 27, 2020, https://www.nasa.gov/audience/forstudents/k-4/stories/nasa-knows/what-is-a-spacewalk-k4.html.

Chapter 4

1. Definitions, s.v. "adoration," accessed November 2, 2020, https://www.definitions.net/definition/adoration.

Chapter 6

1. "Words of Thanks in the Bible," November 1, 2003, Jews for Jesus, https://jewsforjesus.org/publications/newsletter/newsletter-nov-2003/words-of-thanks-in-the-bible.

Chapter 7

1. Vocabulary.com, s.v. "supplicate," accessed November 2, 2020, https://www.vocabulary.com/dictionary/supplicate.
2. BibleHub, s.v. "*suntéreó*," accessed November 2, 2020, https://biblehub.com/greek/4933.htm.

Chapter 9

1. C. S. Lewis, *The Screwtape Letters* (San Francisco: Harper SanFrancisco, 1996), 60–61.

2. Frank E. Gaebelein, general editor, *The Expositor's Bible Commentary, vol. 7* (Grand Rapids, MI: Zondervan, 1985), 46, 59–60.

Chapter 10

1. Jill Dougherty, "U.S. Blames Sudan's President for Darfur 'Catastrophe,'" CNN, March 18, 2009, http://edition.cnn.com/2009/WORLD/africa/03/17/us.sudan/index.html.

Chapter 12

1. In communication with the author. Name withheld for security purposes.
2. Sun Tzu, *The Art of War*, Project Gutenberg, accessed January 8, 2021, http://www.gutenberg.org/files/132/132-h/132-h.htm.
3. Sun Tzu, *The Art of War.*

Conclusion

1. The Martin Luther King, Jr Center, "There comes a time when silence is betrayal…," Twitter, May 29, 2020, https://twitter.com/thekingcenter/status/1266435563097374720?lang=en. See also David Emery, "Did MLK Say 'Our Lives Begin to End the Day We Become Silent'?," Snopes, January 16, 2017, https://www.snopes.com/fact-check/mlk-our-lives-begin-to-end/.

john f. hannah
MINISTRIES

www.johnfhannah.com

A husband, speaker, and author, Pastor John F. Hannah is a voice uniquely crafted for this era. As a staunch community leader and world-renowned evangelist, Pastor Hannah has traveled from Chicago's local communities to international platforms throughout Africa, Australia, and Malaysia. Whether near or far, Pastor Hannah uses his God-given wit, intuitive nature, and calming demeanor to help transform lives for the kingdom of God.

Known for his innate ability to root practical advice in biblical truth, Pastor Hannah has been called upon to offer insight alongside the likes of Steve Harvey and Bishop T. D. Jakes on multiple occasions. From hosting a self-titled, nationally syndicated radio show to a viral podcast trending across digital media, he has had an undeniable impact. The author of two best-selling books, *What to Do While You're Waiting* and *Desperate for Jesus*, Pastor Hannah has returned with his junior release expounding on the necessity of prayer, *Just Pray.*

@pastorhannah

@pastorjhannah

John F. Hannah Ministries

info@jfhministries.com

www.JohnFHannah.com

Made in the USA
Las Vegas, NV
14 April 2021

21281337R00125